Inner Healing: God's Great Assurance

Theodore E. Dobson

PAULIST PRESS
New York/Ramsey/Toronto

Library of Congress
Catalog Card Number: 78-65129

ISBN: 0-8091-2161-1

Published by Paulist Press
Editorial Office: 1865 Broadway, New York, N.Y. 10023
Business Office: 545 Island Road, Ramsey, N.J. 07446

Printed and bound in the
United States of America

INNER HEALING:
GOD'S GREAT ASSURANCE

Contents

Part One

The Dynamics of Healing

I. Life Can Be Healing 3

II. The Healing Power of God 31

III. What Is the Prayer of Loving Faith? 59

IV. How To Pray the Prayer of Loving Faith 88

Part Two

Healing the Inner Person

V. The Need for Inner Healing—
The Human Situation 123

VI. The Beginning of Inner Healing—
Discovering Life in Christ 152

VII. The Fulfillment of Inner Healing—
Forgiveness and Love 173

VIII. A Prayer for Inner Healing 197

Acknowledgements

This book could not have been written without the help and support of many beautiful people. First among them is my devoted typist, Madeleine Streich, whose careful work helped me greatly. Also, I want to thank those who read the manuscript in its early stages and made important contributions and suggestions: Kathleen Molish, Dennis Linn, S.J., Matthew Linn, S.J., Barbara Shlemon, Francis MacNutt, O.P., Morton Kelsey, and Msgr. Harry Koenig. Third, I want to thank the people who gave me the day-to-day emotional support I needed to finish the task when it became difficult: Rev. Philip Dedic, Nick and Bernadette Perrino, and Dan and Lu Smuskiewicz. Finally I owe deep thanks to my parents, Ted and Ruth Dobson, whose pride in my work sustains me in all I do.

To my Mother, Ruth,
who planted in me
the love of words
and the desire to write,

and to the Miracle Lady,
who helped me learn
so much of what I know
and whose constant encouragement
helped to write this book

Part One

The Dynamics of Healing

Chapter I
Life Can Be Healing

God wills life and health for all people. This is God's general stance toward all of us who are his creatures. It was difficult for me to believe this statement when I first heard it, especially with all the experience I had with problems, illness, and pain in my own life, not to speak of the lives of the many people I know. But it is true. "I came that they may have life, and have it abundantly," Jesus said (Jn. 10:10).

That is a difficult proclamation to take literally. It is one that we can easily equivocate, water down, or explain away, as indeed I did for many years whenever I heard or read it. Its simplicity is threatening; our first reaction to it often is that Jesus could not have meant it as it stands. And yet, nowhere do we find him qualifying it—there are no "ifs," "buts" or "maybes" attached to it. It is a statement made for anyone who has ears to hear it.

The easiest way that I found not to pay attention to the real meaning of this verse was to say that it must refer only to spiritual life, i.e., to read it as a promise of abundant grace and life after death. By separating spiritual life from the rest of living (physical, emotional, and intellectual life), I could avoid confronting the possibility that Jesus had anything to say about the ordinary problems I faced day after day, including my physical and emotional illnesses. "Abundant life" was something for a later time, or for another plane of living—an abstract, super-rational, and ethereal plane.

In my attempt to discover the real meaning of Jesus' words, however, it seems that I had moved farther away from his intention. For while the distinction among physical, emo-

3

tional, intellectual, and spiritual life made sense to me, such
thinking was most uncommon in the Hebraic culture of Jesus'
time. A man steeped in Jewish thought as Jesus was could not
separate one level of life from another; this kind of thinking
came from the Greeks, not from the Jews. In the Jewish culture the word "life" was all-encompassing; it referred to all
levels of life. And how real that approach is! Which of us can
look inside ourselves or any living creature and actually point
to the place where physical life ends and emotional, intellectual, or spiritual life begins? These are categories of
thought, not of reality.

While in my thinking, then, it is common to distinguish
among different levels of life, in Jesus' culture it was not
common—indeed, it was virtually impossible—to com-
partmentalize life into different categories. Therefore, the
probability that in talking about abundant life Jesus or the
author of the Gospel, St. John, was referring only to spiritual
life, grace, or life after death is slight. The more probable
meaning is that our common day-to-day lives can be filled by
him with an abundance of every good thing.

However, it is our knowledge and experience of life that
no such abundance is ours. For most of us, at least, our lives
are filled with the opposite of abundant goodness—sickness
and disease, problems, emotional turmoil, phobias, anxieties,
confusion, neuroses, bitterness and resentment, hatred, selfishness. Jesus came into a world whose life revolved then as it
does today around these realities, and yet he said that the
context of our lives could change. These evils and limitations
do not have to be the reality—abundant life could be the
reality.

The questions we have the right to put to him then, are:
How is this transformation to be accomplished, and how can
we participate in abundant life?

These are the very questions that the Gospels were written to answer. The Gospels tell the life story of Jesus, but they

also tell much more than that. As histories, as a matter of fact, they are mediocre reference, since they do not even agree with each other on basic data. Rather than being historical works, the Gospels were written to tell people how to enter the life of Jesus, how to let him be a part of their lives, and how to let him mend the brokenness of their lives. In other words, they were written as documents of faith—documents which inspire our faith in Jesus and which help us to attain the goal of faith.

Furthermore, the meaning of the word Gospel is "Good News." The Gospels tell the Good News of the coming of Jesus into the world and the reconciliation that his life was between God and man. The very nature of that Good News, then, and the way Jesus presents it should be a great help to us in our search for the answers to our questions about how to participate in the abundant life Jesus promised.

The Witness of the Gospel of Mark

As a vehicle to look at some of these issues, I would like to turn to the Gospel of Mark. The reason I want to look at this particular Gospel is its simplicity—in sixteen chapters it presents the essence of the Gospel message. The Scripture scholars also tell us that this Gospel is one of the earliest forms of the Gospel message, that this book is one of the first testimonies of faith of the Church that the apostles formed. In other words, the content of this Gospel formed and also reflected the very faith that the apostles lived and taught. It witnesses to the living attitudes and practices of faith in the lives of the people who were closest to Jesus' ministry. As we look at this Gospel, then, we can ask ourselves how the apostles and the early Church faced the question that we face: "How can we participate in abundant life?"

Jesus appears at the very beginning of the Gospel and

makes an announcement, "The kingdom of God is close at hand. Repent, and believe the Good News." The Good News is what we want to believe in; it is this Good News that will bring us abundant life. But Jesus is enigmatic, secretive. He does not say what the Good News is. In our day of newspapers, news reports all day long on television, and radio stations whose entire purpose and format is to bring news, we tend to think of news as words or ideas that convey to us something we did not know before. Jesus surely does not help us with this kind of news. He does not even say what we are to believe in. He merely announces that we are to repent and believe, and he moves on.

The word "repent" in his announcement might give us a clue. The word originally used in the Greek manuscript is *metanoia*, which means "change your heart" or "change your ways." Still, that is not much help when we are excited to believe and find abundant life. So we move on and look further. In the very next section Jesus does teach, but what he said is not recorded. All we know is that he taught with authority and was favorably received by the people. We read that Jesus drives out an unclean spirit from a man, that he cures Peter's mother-in-law, and then he cures so many that the number was too great to count and relate individually.

We see, then, that immediately following his admonition to "repent and believe" Jesus does not preach this Good News and explain it; rather, he performs many miracles. Yet, this segment of the Gospel concludes with Jesus saying to his disciples, "Let us go elsewhere . . . so that I can preach there too. . . ." Preach what? He announces "Good News," heals many people, and then wants to go to other places to "preach there too." But the Gospel narrative has not recorded a word of preaching up to this point. Either the author is leaving out of his book some vitally important material, namely, the content of this Good News we are supposed to believe in, or there is a message in Jesus' actions that we have not as yet understood.

Once again, however, we do not find Jesus preaching about anything important; rather we find him healing. Jesus heals a man who has a withered hand and there is another account of Jesus healing many. Following these accounts, we read of Jesus choosing the Twelve, of Jesus' relatives who think he is "out of his mind," and of the scribes and Pharisees accusing him of casting out demons by Satan's power. This last episode is especially interesting because Jesus is being persecuted for showing power and healing. Finally, the third chapter concludes with Jesus' "mother and brothers" coming to see him.

Up to this point in the narrative we have seen Jesus do several things. He has made his announcement, "Repent, and believe the Good News"; he has cured many illnesses and showed power by casting out demons as well; he has done some things that begin to establish the kingdom of God, e.g., choosing the disciples, declaring that the kingdom is for sinners and not the self-righteous, and establishing some spiritual laws for living in the kingdom. And we have seen some people's reactions to him: the crowds are awestruck and praise God, the demons shriek, the Pharisees and Herodians are angry and plot against him, those who are healed are grateful, his relatives disown him, and his mother and brothers visit him.

Many events have taken place in these three chapters and many issues have been raised. But one element is noticeably absent—preaching. Jesus has not yet preached his Good News. We still do not know what it is. Or do we? Have we missed what Mark has been trying to say? When an author writes a book we can assume he has a message and a plan by which to convey that message. If by the end of the third chapter in a book that comprises sixteen chapters the author has not stated his theme, he would be a poor writer indeed. It could be that Mark has already said many times what the Good News is.

But if he has, we know that the Good News cannot be words but rather actions, for that is what these three chapters have mainly been relating. Many people today see the Good News in terms of what Jesus taught, the moral pronouncements and spiritual laws he revealed. But apparently Mark did not see Jesus as viewing the Good News that way, or by this point in his book he would have related the Good News that Jesus is announcing in terms of a great teaching.

The first teaching of any length or importance in the Gospel of Mark begins in the fourth chapter, the parable of the sower. This parable is a familiar one; it tells of a sower sowing his seed in various types of soil and what happens to the seed when it tries to grow in different conditions. Then later as Jesus is explaining the parable to his apostles, he tells them that the seed in the parable represents the word of God.

The Word and the Gospel

Here we might have a clue to the answers we seek. The word of God surely has a strong relationship to the Good News of Jesus. Indeed, God's word is Good News to mankind, for his word liberates, transforms, and renews. It could be that from this parable and from the meaning of the phrase "word of God" to the Hebrew mind we can find out what the Good News is and how to let abundant life into our own experience.

First, let us look at the Hebrew notion of God's word. The word of God is an image from the antiquity of the Jewish religion. The prophets especially taught about what the word of God in reality was. Twentieth-century man thinks of words as merely a number of letters of the alphabet put together, representing a sound which describes a particular thing or idea. The reality of the world for us is not in words but in the things they describe. However, it was not so for the ancient

Hebrew. Words for him had a reality all their own. And the word of God had a unique reality: it was a dynamic principle of action. *It accomplished what it said.*

For example, in Genesis we read: "God said, 'Let there be light,' and there was light" (Gn 1:3). Just by God's *saying* it, light came to be. God's *word* created. Through the prophets God taught us that he will not let his word come back to him empty (e.g., Is 55:11). He is saying that, unlike humans who say many things that do not actually happen (how often has the theme of "empty promises" alone occupied the minds of men and women in literature throughout the ages), whatever God says *will* happen just because he has said it.

But what exactly is the word that Jesus is speaking about in this parable? What is the word that Jesus has been sowing all around the countryside of Galilee? What is the Good News that he has been announcing?

He has not taught it because no teaching is necessary. For Jesus *is* the word of God. *He* is the Good News. His presence on earth heralds a new age of peace between God and man. His very presence brings God's love which heals some, confronts others, and angers still others who then want to destroy him. And that seems to be Mark's reason for not revealing the Good News in a teaching. Mark knew the message he was conveying. He was telling the life story of the man who was and is Good News.

Even in our theology and in our piety we call Jesus the "word of God," the perfect utterance and reflection of the Father. Jesus is the "word" that the Father speaks to mankind in the new covenant. Only a person could be the Father's word, because only a person could speak through action his fullest love to mankind. And the Father wanted a word so loving, so hopeful, so beautiful that only a divine-human person could enact it.

In what actions, then, did Jesus show himself as the loving word of God? Let us look back to the end of the first chapter of Mark when the disciples find Jesus and tell him everyone is looking for him. Jesus says he must go all around to other towns and preach. Then Mark says, "And he went all through Galilee, preaching in their synagogues and casting out devils." Following this statement are the stories of preaching, two cures, one of a leper and the other of a paralytic. The "word" Jesus was speaking, the seed he was sowing in his actions was love—caring about the hurts of the people he met. But he did not care in an empty way; he cared for them by *healing* them, by using his love and his power to take from them the problems of their lives. The word Jesus came to say to mankind was unity between God and man, peace between God and man, love of God for man.

And looking over the Gospel as a unit, as one story, we find Jesus' life *doing* this very "word"—reconciling, making people whole, making people free. That is the Good News, and Jesus did it for us in his life, as well as in his death and resurrection. Jesus is the word proclaiming that people do not have to go to God, that God has come to people and God chooses to live with us and in us. Nor is God doing this in a purposeless way but rather to share with us his own power and victory over all that would limit and hurt, over all that has broken our world and broken us as well in the process. This is why Jesus is curing and more than teaching—to show the power of God, and even more importantly to show that God uses his power to make us whole, not to hurt us, or, even worse, to have no effect on us.

Jesus, then, is the Gospel to believe in; Jesus is the abundant life we seek; Jesus is the Good News we want to hear and see. And we can hear and see this Good News through all the different ways Jesus brings peace to a world at war with itself and all the different ways Jesus heals a world broken and crumbling around and within us. Healing which brings freedom, which is a sign of love, is inextricably woven into the Gospel. Without the healing love of Jesus touching and changing the lives of men, relieving their pain, the Good News becomes good advice, or, worse, bad news.

The Good News in One Particular Life

This approach to the Gospel has brought God's power and love into my life. My own experience of healing has been a process of growth, pain, freedom, and love that has stretched out through my whole life. During the first twenty-five years of my life I did not see the elements of God's love in or around me, not very well, at least; but through the eyes of today I can see how God was using each experience for me.

Let me quickly add, also, that I did not feel my experience to be remarkable as I was going through it. It was a life as we all have known—with highs and lows, with its own share of sadness and pain and rejection, with much confusion in growing up, etc.

I grew up a lonely child, feeling afraid, rejecting, bristling with anger. As a very small child I had been lively and loving, but a darkness came over me during my early years that lasted a long time. In that darkness I attempted to function as well as possible, but I felt as if I were fighting to get out of quicksand. Contact with the outer world never seemed to be made. I felt as if I were lost in my own world; I could see others in the world outside of me and I could watch them interact—how I longed to be among them—but I could not touch them. I could not touch their inner selves, or, at least, I could not see that I touched them. And my blindness was the result of my anger and rejection. But I saw it entirely as my problem; I felt that I was not made "right"—something essential was missing. Something was wrong with *me* because I could not feel love. How sad I was, and how fearful of everyone else! The more successful others were in the outer world—the world I could not enter no matter how hard I tried—the more I was afraid of their power and the more I resented them for having what I could not have, the warmth of feeling loved.

This is not to say that there were not people around me loving me. I had a mother and a father who had adopted me. So I should have seen their love for me as twice blessed: I was their child and they had chosen me from among others. And around me were my sister, many aunts, uncles, and cousins, grandparents and friends of the family. I had normal opportunities to make friends my own age and to engage in the play and learning of childhood. But I could not enter into these people and experiences. I felt outside and alone.

And so I became an expert at rejection. Since I felt rejected—although at that age I could not put that label on my feelings—I learned how to reject someone before he or she could reject me. If I had to be alone, at least I could be strong, I thought. And in this way I made a more and more conscious decision to be separate, to reject, and not to love or be loved.

There was also, however, a positive side. As I mentioned earlier, before the age of three I was a happy child, alert, fun to be with, ready to play and relate. When I grew quieter and darker, I had to find some area of excellence, some area in which I could use my left-over energy and experience success. So I concentrated on my studies and being in the top echelon of my class wherever I was. This way I always gained attention and a type of respect from others, and these responses helped me to cope with life as cold as it was inside of me. But because I was never number one in academic standing, because there were always a few ahead of me, I sometimes found reason to reject even that part of myself.

It was in the high school years that I felt things beginning to move in the right direction. But I did not come to know Jesus in a personal way until many years later. I had had several experiences of the Holy Spirit filling me with peace and love during my childhood and adolescence, and I had a great interest in the Lord and enough faith to lead me into the seminary, and the formative influences on my life had been of high quality; but meeting the Lord is such a personal thing. I experienced it as something I was driven to, the only positive resolution to all the problems and desperation of my life until then.

It was the spring of 1970, and I was in New York City at the age of 23. I had completed two years of graduate work in theology and was in a clinical training program, the goal of which was to help seminarians learn skills in ministering to people in hospitals and other crisis situations. I came to New York a sad Christian—sad emotionally and theologically. Emotionally, the year preceding my time in New York had been the first consistent breaking through of light in over ten years; but while this was encouraging, I still was a rather sad creature to know, rejecting myself and others, full of anger at the world, dependent, fearful.

My theological state reflected my emotional state; I had become a "modern Christian." Although I had been well schooled in orthodox teaching, sound methodology, and the works of theology's great writers, I responded most to the watered-down kind of faith that was popular in the late 1960's—God is not transcendent but rather totally immanent; Jesus was the fullest revelation of God but when he died God died with him; Jesus' main task was to show us the right moral path by which to live good lives; therefore, prayer was at best an exercise in self-understanding and at worst was utter non-sense.

My position in New York was as a chaplain intern in a general hospital, and in ministering as a chaplain I had an experience that was to change all that I have been relating about myself and my problems, and was to mark my entire future. One day I was called on to talk with a patient who was not on one of my assigned floors. The nurses on duty that particular night felt it was an emergency that a chaplain talk to this man. Since I was on night duty I came. When I arrived I found out why the nurses were so upset. This was a very religious hospital with a rule that every patient should be visited by a chaplain during his or her stay, but this patient was near to death from stomach cancer and no chaplain had ever visited him. Our conversation was brief; but the next day when he died I was called to recite the prayers for the dead over him since my visit the night before had made me "his" chaplain.

When we had begun our chaplain intern program we had been advised that some situation such as this one could easily happen while we were on duty in the hospital; our supervisor had recommended that we choose beforehand the prayers we wanted to pray so that we would be prepared at the moment the situation arose. So, armed with my prayer book and "scared out of my mind," I went to his room.

This man had had a lonely death. He had no family, and his few friends had stopped visiting him halfway into his hospital stay. His situation was pitiful and I felt for him deeply. The physical pain of the final days for a victim of cancer of the stomach is excruciating, resulting in a sad response from the nurses of being upset and not spending much time with him. As I walked into the room two male attendants were pulling the white sheet over his face, and when they saw me they hurriedly fled. I was alone with my friend.

I began praying. The prayers I had chosen, strangely enough, were prayers filled with a rich faith in God. As I was speaking the words that were in front of me, I said to myself, "Ted, either you are doing the most important thing you have ever done in your life—commending the soul of a faithful Christian of fifty-eight years to his eternal Father—or you are doing the most ridiculous thing you have ever done—saying meaningless words, with no one here even to be comforted by them, to a corpse. Now what are you doing? Do you believe or don't you?"

In the struggle of that moment, the Truth I had been looking for all my life found me. God reached out and touched me. It was a physical sensation, like a hand firmly pressing on my head. I felt as if I would faint, but my first reaction was to prevent that by sheer will power. I concentrated on the words I was saying as the one link I had to reality, and the awareness drove through me profoundly: I do believe.

As soon as the last syllable of the prayer had left my lips, I turned, left the room, and navigated my way down the hall somewhat wobbly like a drunk. An elevator trip and a walk of a few yards left me in the chapel. There I knelt and sat and sobbed for nearly a half hour. I cried for the man whose death was so lonely and painful, I cried out of my pain at first praying over someone who had just died, and I cried over the release I felt within me, although I could not have said at that time what it was, where it came from, or even what it meant.

Later on that day, life took on its more ordinary contours and feelings; everything seemed to return emotionally and spiritually to what it used to be. Something had been released, but I did not know what it was. But a few days afterward, and once again every week for the rest of the spring and all during the summer of that year, one thought quietly recurred in moments of reflection: "I wonder if I could ever live in the faith I had for that short time." Each time the thought left as quickly as it came.

Wonder I did until I returned to the seminary. There I signed up for a seminar course called "Reflections on Pastoral Experience: Ministry in the City." Early on in the course I brought this experience from the previous spring for all to look at and learn from. To help me understand what had happened, the professor suggested I read William James' work *Varieties of Religious Experience*. In the book I found that not only had I had a religious experience, but also that it was a classical one. The book provided the intellectual framework I had needed to accept my experience as a reality and not just as a figment of an emotional state. That book made it possible for me to say to myself, "God is real. He touched me."

The Spirit Is Released

The following spring I was ordained a deacon and I began to work in a parish where I met some people who were interested in investigating the Charismatic Renewal in the Catholic Church. They asked me to come to a prayer meeting with them as a friend and as a pastor. My own reaction to the Renewal had been a long-standing negative one from the first time I had read about it in *Time* magazine in the late 1960's. The people involved in prayer meetings seemed to me to be over-emotional, theologically naive, and foolish, especially in their belief in miracles. I, of course, like any common-sensical twentieth-century Christian, "knew" that miracles were not possible. But behind that opinion was a strong personal attitude: I had lived and struggled with my problems for years and had found, if not peace, at least some answers; and if I could do it, so could everyone else. Therefore, not only were miracles impossible, they were also simply not needed.

But because my friends asked me I went along with them, mostly looking forward to spending some time with them after the prayer meeting was over. What I found, however, was entirely different from what I expected. I remember having difficulty finding the place in which the prayer meeting was held and being led to the room late by the pastor of the parish. Then, the next time we came, we entered just as the meeting was beginning; all the people were standing with their arms raised singing to the Lord. I stood there for a moment and was almost pushed back by an indefinable power in the room—it was so strong I could feel it. And I said to myself spontaneously, without even making a decision about it, "I don't know what it is they have, but whatever it is I want it."

Three weeks later I knew God was calling me to a new

kind of relationship with him. Everything that was taught and witnessed to at these meetings—everything—cut through me as if it were a knife. I had never heard the word of God preached with such authority; I had never felt God's power so personally. Then at my fourth prayer meeting I committed my life to Jesus Christ and asked the Holy Spirit to take over in my life and fill me with his gifts.

Soon after this experience some friends of mine who had been attending prayer meetings for some time asked me to meet a lady they had come to know in a neighboring prayer group. Her name was Barbara Shlemon, and my friends told me that she was very excited to hear that I had personally experienced the Lord. What I did not know about Barbara at this time was that she had an active healing ministry and that one of her deepest longings was to see priests become involved in the Renewal and especially in healing, because, as she saw it, priests are given the charism of healing at their ordination to help them in their ministry to the sick and troubled of heart.

I went to one of the prayer meetings she attended—about one hundred people were there—and I was deeply touched by the love I felt in that room. After the meeting my friends introduced me to Barbara who looked directly into my eyes and said with a simple, spiritual love, "The Lord is going to use you greatly in the healing ministry." "Oh?" I responded. "What's that?"

Six months later I was to find out, not on the giving but rather on the receiving end of that ministry. I had joined this particular prayer group as a weekly member; and one day when I was talking with a friend in the prayer group about some problems I was experiencing in the parish, he suggested that I talk with Barbara, because he knew that she had helped many people through counseling and prayer. At that point in my life I did not know whom else I could trust to give me sound spiritual advice, so I asked Barbara if I could see her sometime.

That visit to her house is one I will never forget. By the

time I had arrived there I had already "figured out" my own problem—I did not have enough faith, hope, or love. I sat down with Barbara over a cup of tea at her kitchen table and told her my situation and my diagnosis of it. Her gentle comment was, "I think your problems come from a little farther back in your life than that. Could you tell me something about yourself?"

This was the last question I wanted to hear. But the look in her eyes was so gentle yet persistent that I began to talk. "Well, if you have to know the whole story, I guess I should begin by telling you that I'm adopted."

So I quickly outlined the story of my life as I saw it, telling her of this happy person locked up inside loneliness, feelings of rejection, pessimism, and fear; and I told her of the painful experiences and relationships of my life. Her response was beautiful. Without blaming me or anyone else, and without making me feel threatened in any way, she said, "I see one word written across all of your life, and it's written in giant capital letters. That word is 'rejection'—you have felt rejected as you turned every corner of your life, but it hasn't been anyone's fault. It all began with your adoption—you felt rejected by your natural mother when she gave you up, and you've seen every painful experience since then through that one."

"Barbara," I said, quite discouraged, "I've worked through my adoption already. I've known I'm adopted since I was three and I accept it. It isn't a problem anymore."

"Well, let me pray with you anyway," she said.

"But I have real problems with real people in my life right now. Can't we pray about them?" I said anxiously.

"Surely we can," she soothed me. "But we have to pray about your adoption, too."

"But Barbara," I pleaded, "I have problems with people in the present enough to take up all the time we have."

"Let's pray," she said, and she said it with such a quiet firmness that I knew what I would do. She reached her hands across the table and took my hands in hers. While she closed her eyes and bowed her head I resolved to endure however long it would take just so that I could get out of there. I was entirely uninvolved in what she was saying and doing—or so I thought. I looked around the room and noticed the pattern on the wallpaper; then I saw the breakfast dishes in the sink and wondered why she was not keeping her house instead of wasting my time praying about some nonsensical thing that happened many years ago. My reaction was typical enough, I guess, for one who is new to this kind of prayer, inner healing prayer; for I did not see how the past could have such a tremendous effect on the present or how the unconscious could keep a memory so active and vital even though the conscious had resolved the issue years ago, nor did I see what prayer could do about it anyway.

But something began to happen. I did not understand it at the time, and even today I do not fully comprehend how the prayer for inner healing touches a person so deeply, but I began to cry. I was hearing her words from a place deep within me, a place I had never touched before. Barbara asked Jesus to enter all the months I had spent in my mother's womb and all the feelings which she had—which I also felt because I was a part of her and she communicated them to me—because of the fact of my presence within her and because of the fact that she had to give me up. She spoke to me in the name of my natural mother and father and told me they were sorry for giving me life and then having to give me away, but that it was the most loving thing they could do for me. And I forgave them. Then I spoke to my adopted parents and told them how sorry I was for taking out on them the way I felt toward my natural mother and father, and I opened myself to the love my adopted parents had tried to give me all the years of my life.

What a tremendous release this was for me! Within a few weeks after the prayer it seemed as if layers and layers of darkness had been lifted from me. The gloomy atmosphere that I had sensed constantly disappeared, and the feelings of rejection I had always experienced slowly began to be replaced with the love that my wonderful Mom and Dad had for me, and the love Jesus felt for me too. It was a first step, an opening up. From that point on my spiritual life seemed to me to move into high gear. My relationship with Jesus and my faith in him began to take wings.

Seven or eight months later, in May 1973, Barbara suggested that I attend a workshop on healing that her friend, Father Francis MacNutt, was giving with two other teachers. Somewhat reluctantly I agreed to go—reluctantly because, even though I had experienced healing and I had seen many healings, some quite dramatic, I still was not convinced that it was real. When I reflect on this time in my life, it is not difficult for me to understand the skepticism that many people have when they first are exposed to direct healing by the Lord. My own skepticism ran deep, but because I tested each question and sought convincing experience of healing for myself, my commitment to believe in the Lord's power to heal now runs just as deep.

I drove to that workshop with a friend, protesting throughout the eight-hour trip that I did not know why I was going to it since I did not truly believe in healing. I allowed myself to think that I was going as a favor to Barbara. But such was not the case. At the workshop I heard the message of God's healing power preached, and, more importantly, I found the healing power of the Lord in my own life freeing me from my greatest fears and anxieties, so much so that I looked and felt like a new man. Exteriorly my face glowed and my eyes shone with the peace of Christ; within I felt as though my whole body had been renewed. I felt quiet and calm but not alone, and I *knew* that God loved me because he acted on my behalf with obvious power at the time he was needed the most. And so, while I went to this week-long experience doubting the reality of healing, I came home preaching that healing is at the very center of the Gospel message.

Soon after returning home my public ministry of healing began. And my own healing continued. Layer upon layer of negative feelings were resolved, each with a lot of prayer and a lot of love; consequently I found that the Lord was in my life in many new and helpful ways; prayer had invited him into each of these areas of my life to accomplish his saving act within me. Soon I found that God's salvation is not some abstract thing that God gives to us, but that he saves us from each fear, each limitation, each hurt, disgrace, and confusion of our lives. He will save each part of us if we invite him into each part of us through prayer. Our bodies are included in that promise of his, along with our emotions, minds and spirits. He has saved each part of us already on the cross, and he wants to reveal to us right here and now the power of his sacrifice by freeing us in every way that is possible and good for us.

I hope that in describing these changes I have not given the impression that they were instantaneous, absolute, and constant. As with any normal change within the human personality they happened slowly and, indeed, are still happening. The weaknesses that were in my personality, to a great extent, will always be a part of me; however, the strength of Christ now shines through them. Christ has done for me many things I could never have done for myself—he broke the dark cloud cover of depression; he lighted the way on the dangerous path of my unconscious fears and hatred of myself; he opened doors to entirely new approaches to relating with people and to being a part of and not apart from his creation; he comforted the hurting parts of me and healed them so that they became strong enough to function again; he released within me my imprisoned power to care for others and express my care in ways others could feel; he gave me the grace of forgiveness so that the resentments and hurts of my life could find resolution; he gave me the gift of faith.

But he has never done for me anything I could do for

myself. And I am sure his reason for leaving those things to me was and is to preserve my dignity and to help me to mature. But how carefully, intricately, gently, and lovingly he has laid before me his plan for my recovery and my participation in the healing of the world, one step at a time.

A little over a year later, in August 1974, I received my first invitation to teach outside of my parish and/or prayer group situation. Jesus then helped me reflect on my own experiences of growth and on the lives of those I had touched through my healing ministry to glean from them the truth of faith and the power of love that he wants me to convey as clearly and as gently as I can.

Yet I had not learned the entire preliminary lesson of God's love. The next year and a half were filled with much work and many personal problems. The mistakes I made in new relationships, the fears that still lingered in my half-healed personality, the feeling that often I was in water over my head led me to want to hide from God, and I chose to hide behind an age-old mask of the hard-working priest. I worked and worried almost continuously in order to earn God's love and the love of others because I did not believe I could be loved for myself alone. Even the affirmation others gave to my work and to me as a person I interpreted as a pressure, because I still had not let the Lord touch a deeper level of fear which told me that people did not love me for who I am, but rather that they must love me for what I do for them—my priestly work and my healing ministry. I believed I was loved, but I did not see the real motive of those who loved me.

And so I drove myself—right to the point of nervous exhaustion. When the doctor told me that for the next six to eight weeks I should not do any work aside from the most basic of parish duties, I fearfully followed his orders. It was in the quiet of the time that followed that I began to sense the depth of the concern and love of many people around me and the Truth broke through. "They love you for who you are," the Lord said to me through my experience. "You are not presently doing a thing for them yet they are still concerned for you. And my Father loves you in the very same way."

It was a time when my whole life stopped and much of it collapsed around me, but it was one of the most beautiful and creative times of my life. I found that what was collapsing and dying was the "old me"—the afraid me, the rigid me, the defensive me, the grasping and desperate me. All the parts of me that I never liked I suddenly saw as non-essential, and I also saw that I had the choice to let them go. I knew that if I had the courage to let them go and feel a little lost and "identity-less" for a while, a new man would arise and my dreams of being a free, self-determining man under the Lord's direction would be much closer to realization. And so I let go, and it began happening. Engaging the assistance and stability of a professional counselor for a period of about eight months, and always with the help of friends, I was able to walk into a future of new potentialities and new freedoms.

The Process of Healing

Throughout these few years of my life in which I have been consciously aware of the healing love of the Lord, the most important fact I have discovered is that healing is a process, and it is a process under God's direction that makes life abundant. It seems to me that many people cannot understand or accept healing stories about God's power and love because they view healing as "a" healing—a discrete moment in time, separate from all other moments, in which God intervenes and contradicts a law of nature to accomplish some unusual goal. My experience has been exactly the opposite of this attitude. As I have seen and felt it, God's healing love as it enters the life of a human being is a force that stimulates growth and change; God and his love become a normal part of every day and of every part of that person. The power of God's presence to change and heal is released through faith and love, so that this healing power releases natural processes where they have been blocked or slowed down. For, it seems to me, God put the world together in such a way that it is natural for healing to happen. Abundant life is man's goal in heaven, and we find a taste of it here on earth as we begin to live in the kingdom of God through faith and love.

I have found that healing is a process that leads to certain attitudes of body, mind, emotions, and spirit, and that these attitudes can bring great health and happiness in a person's life. First and foremost, real healing from God is a process that leads to compassion.

Compassion is something for which we all search in our society. It is not a value that ranks high in the world's system, and so there are many things that we are led to believe by the opinion-makers of our society that destroy compassionate feelings and behavior. But that does not destroy our need for compassion. We all look for acceptance and love, for under-standing of our own uniqueness. When we do not find these qualities in the people around us and in ourselves we become more and more desperate in our search and/or we become hardened inside, trusting and growing and enjoying very little.

The compassion to which healing leads comes from the peace that healing brings, a peace whose source is God him-self. Peace fills us when we are assured in the heart of our hearts that the God of all things, the Creator of the universe, the Lord of all time, the Source of all life, loves me, and that he loves me enough to use his massive, infinite power for my welfare and to make me happy. The experience of God's love brings the peace that the world cannot give.

Firmly secured in true peace, I am free to be compassionate—to be concerned about another person's wor-ries for a time, to lose my "self" or to die to myself that I might dedicate my love and talents to the life of another. To the degree to which I know this peace I will have a consistent wellspring of compassion from which to draw. To the extent that my heart does not know the peace that comes from God's love I will not have the energy or the time to help others out of a simple concern for them because I will spend my energy on my own needs and pursuits.

The peace that comes from healing seems to me to be a necessary pre-condition to following the Gospel commands to love our brothers and sisters in the Lord. This peace opens me up to see God's possibilities for my life. I do not always have to be looking out for myself, for God has and will continue to look out for me; therefore, I can relax and dedicate myself to loving as Jesus asks me to. And compassion becomes more a part of me.

This peace which the world cannot give also frees me from the necessity of judging other people, especially when my tendency to judge others comes from a need to build myself up by putting other people down. As the peace that comes from God's healing love takes over my life, I find I have less and less need to build myself up, to put others down, or to put myself down. God's peace stabilizes me and relaxes me; it equalizes my view of things. I begin to see the pain out of which I was functioning, but I see it from a distance because it is being healed. I begin to see that I used to be hurting so badly in certain areas that I had to build myself up in others so that I would not seem to myself to be a total failure. God's love has healed me so that the pain changes shape within me—it no longer cripples me but rather it has been healed to the point where it becomes a creative source within me (an example of God's strength being shown through my weakness).

From that point within me I can begin to help others. I will love them out of my understanding of my own need to be loved. I will be gentle with them because I will be sensitive not to hurt them in the way I was hurt. I will respect their uniqueness out of a hard-earned awareness of my own uniqueness and the freedom I need to be and to become and to make mistakes. Truly I will become a wounded healer. I will be touching others with a sensitive compassion whose home base in me will be the wounds in my life that the Lord has touched and healed. Thus the loving touch which I will offer to the world will also be the Lord's loving and healing touch, for he will reach through my wounds into the lives of many.

And compassion will become more a part of my way of life. My compassion for others begins most truly and grows most quickly when it is nourished on a profound compassion for myself. My own tendency and the tendency of many with whom I have shared is to be too hard on ourselves. Whether it shows itself in a lack of forgiveness for past sins, a lack of understanding of failures, a lack of acceptance of limitations, a need to be perfect or suffer the consequences of self-criticism, a drive to achieve, a feeling of general incompetence, or one of a hundred other manifestations, this tendency to be rough and overdemanding of ourselves is often the source of many of our problems, not the least of which is our tendency to be demanding, unforgiving, un-understanding, and unaccepting of others.

Some people react to this inhuman burden of responsibility for all negative elements in their past by giving up entirely and being totally undemanding on themselves even in areas where a balanced amount of pressure would be helpful. Others give in to these tendencies and become, to one degree or another, depressed, unhappy, morose, and ineffective people. It is only those who see a third way out, a way by which these attitudes are neither accepted nor rejected but rather *healed*, that find their lives developing into the powerful witnesses to the love of the Lord that the Gospel promises for us.

To seek healing for ourselves, then, is a profoundly compassionate act—an act of self-compassion that will bring much hope and love in the lives of the people we touch. And to seek healing for ourselves is not only necessary to begin living a life of Gospel love but also to continue it and to see it through to its completion in our own sanctity. Without some kind of healing for ourselves we cannot be whole or holy.

Second, healing is a process that leads toward individuality. Strengthened in my appreciation of my own worth, I have been able to accept my feelings and my needs more readily. When a person feels under attack from within—an attack that comprises the feelings of guilt and anger which come from painful memories and experiences—his need to be strong can overwhelm his personality to the point that he must deny his feelings and his need for others as signs of weakness. The peace and compassion that the healing power of God introduces into a person's life relaxes him to the point that he understands he does not always need to be strong, that he can accept himself as he is, that he can show his need for others by actually relying on them. Through healing of the inner man, a person can find out that this kind of acceptance is not selfish, only realistic. With this realistic self-acceptance life becomes less burdensome, the depressingly heavy side of life becomes less influential, possibilities and hope abound, and life can begin to feel good, for some for the first time in their lives.

The individuality toward which healing leads also releases my creative potential, my imaginal world—the world of self-discovery, art, imagination, possibilities, new interests, new life-styles, and new ways of relating and playing, as well as the world of love, of hope, and of faith.

In my own life I have seen this potential released as I have found new directions, new freedoms, a renewed belief in myself.

For example, in the last year I have begun to become involved in areas in which I would only allow myself to have a distant interest formerly. My garden blooms outside; my book has been written. I have asserted myself in relationships, finding out to my surprise that friends do not walk away when I express the anger or disappointment I feel in our relationship at a particular time. Because I have been freer to show my negative emotions, I have also become freer to be gentle and kind—a paradox that is not easy to understand until it has been experienced. Most simply phrased, I have taken my life much more into my own hands, I am not so easily pushed around by my own "unacceptable" feelings or by the feelings and actions of others. I feel and act with a greater sense of my freedom and responsibility, my uniqueness, and my dignity as a human being.

Third, I have found that healing is a process that makes me become real and to see my reality. This statement is especially true of the kind of healing called healing of the inner person or "inner healing." For in this kind of emotional healing I begin to accept the truth about myself, not the lies that I have been taught by the world.

For example, when a child is not loved in the way he needs and deserves to be, his response often will be that he thinks he is not a lovable person. This thought, however, is a lie. No child is born unlovable, but many develop unlovable characteristics by being treated in an unloving way. Inner healing uncovers this lie and exposes it for what it is, for through inner healing a person comes to accept that in everything he has ever done and everything that has ever happened to him God has continued to love him. Jesus has been at his side caring for him, ministering to his hurt and forgiving his sin throughout all his life. Little by little he comes to realize that God's love for him is more real than the sin of the world against him, and God's message to him is truer than the world's. Finally he begins to see himself as he is—he begins to see himself through his Creator's eyes.

When I saw these truths taking shape in my own life it became easier to acknowledge and own my feelings. Now I can state my opinion without forcing others to agree on the one hand or letting them step all over it on the other, for I believe in the worth of what I say and am. I find myself becoming simpler and more sincere in my words, my actions, and my prayers; for when I ask myself "Do I really mean it?" I have a greater awareness of the "I" to which I am referring. I have found that love is most basic of the positive emotions. I find that I feel love more and more as my heart becomes simple and as I acknowledge all of my feelings as real. The peace that comes into my heart from simplicity and reality allows love to flow from me ever more naturally.

Also as this has been happening I have found that one of the great longings of my life has been satisfied in ever new and delightful ways—I can feel loved. I noticed how natural it was to feel love from many different people *to the extent and in the way* they wanted to give it during the Christmas season of 1976. As a priest I receive many gifts of different kinds from people in my parish as well as from my family and friendship community. During the Christmas season of 1976 I noticed as I received each gift that I felt and appreciated the feelings of closeness and love with which each gift was given. Each giver was different, each gift was different, and each feeling was different. And I could enjoy every one. Instead of concentrating on the gift and what it was or was not, I felt what the giver was intending, and my own gratitude poured lavishly from my heart. Each gift warmed me; each gift had the potential to fill me with what I need to give to others.

It was not difficult to understand in January 1977 that the same opportunities for gift-giving and gift-receiving go on all year long, and that each day I can receive many gifts to fill up that needy part of me with affirmation and love. And I can do it for others, too. And as I meditate on the tremendous importance of all these little gifts I begin to understand in a small way the meaning of the phrase "the body of Christ."

For as giving and receiving love replace the wasting of energy in fear and anxiety and guilt, I begin to enter into the

reality of Jesus' wholeness. He called it the new and abundant
life that he came to bring us. Through acting as a member of
the body of Christ I begin to see myself as I really am *in Jesus'
eyes*—beautiful though wounded, spotless while weak, forgiven, healed, and whole, the beloved of Jesus, a precious
child of the Father, with the glory of the Spirit's love surrounding me, filling me, dignifying me as a saint. Jesus has
called me into relationship with him, and all through my life I
will be his confidant, his co-worker, his friend, his playmate,
his lover, the receiver of many gifts from him, and the giver of
the gift of myself to him, the only person with whom I would
completely trust a prize so precious as the self I had hidden
and worked so hard to find.

Chapter II
The Healing Power of God

All men and women who call themselves Christian agree that Jesus is our Redeemer. All Christians say that Jesus has saved us from our sins, has lifted the burden of guilt from our shoulders, has paid the price for our disobedience. Jesus has reconciled us to God our Father, we proclaim, so that there is no unpaid debt between us; rather, the "lines of communication" are open and we are free to approach our Father in prayer and love.

Jesus' ministry of reconciliation has taken the rupture between God and man and healed it. Although the work of Jesus on the cross is not usually spoken of as a work of healing, that is indeed what it was. Jesus was mending the broken relationship between God and man; and also he was mending the brokenness within man, the division that each of us finds between our real destiny and what we can attain on our own. Sin had worked to divide man from God and man from himself, and so sin was the conqueror; but in Christ all of sin's effects were undone, and wholeness again became a possibility for mankind.

While all of these are common statements of belief in the Christian churches, and while many individual believers build their personal faith life around them, it seems to be uncommon among some Christians to draw out all these beliefs to their logical conclusions. For example, if Jesus healed us from our sins and saved us, he also saved us from the effects of those sins. Sin brought with it into the world suffering and pain,

31

confusion, darkness of the mind and will, faults and weaknesses, and death. Indeed, every limitation that we feel in the world—and all of them were brought into the world by sin—is like a little death, a death of a part of ourselves that God has created to live and to give life. Death is the only logical conclusion to sin. The life that Jesus came to bring us is God's answer to the death we experience through sin. But since the death we experience is on all levels of existence—emotional, intellectual, physical, and spiritual—so too is the life that Jesus has brought us.

The evidence of this truth is all through Scripture. For example, Isaiah foretold the coming of the Messiah and how he would save mankind in his songs of the suffering servant. These are poetic prophesies scattered throughout the middle of the Book of Isaiah. Let us cite one of them here:

> And yet ours were the *sufferings* he bore,
> ours the *sorrows* he carried.
> But we, we thought of him as someone *punished*,
> struck by God, and *brought low*.
> Yet he was pierced through for our *faults*,
> crushed for our *sins*.
> On him lies a punishment that *brings us peace*,
> and through his wounds *we are healed* (Is 53:3-5; italics mine).

Notice that Isaiah does not refer only to the *sins* from which the Messiah will save his people, but also to sufferings and sorrows, faults and punishments, rejections and depressions. And Isaiah sees the effect of the Messiah's action as bringing us peace and healing us. Isaiah's vision of Jesus' work seems to be quite broad and complete. The Messiah that he sees will bring about a total reconciliation for mankind, and that reconciliation will bring freedom and wholeness to man's being, and healing.

And how realistic that vision is! How realistic is its basic insight and approach! For which one of us feels truly free when only some of our problems are solved? If only a portion of mankind's dilemma would have been dealt with on the cross, we would have cause to wonder. We would wonder how to deal with the rest of our problems; we would wonder about a God who accomplished only half a task; we would wonder how he could love us totally as he says if he only healed us partially. Yet often individuals do wonder about all these things because they wrongly believe that God is only concerned about a part of us, the spiritual part. God's care for us is much bigger than that—it is infinite, eternal, unlimited—and his word to us tells us so over and over again.

In the creation story in Genesis, we learn that the world was made to be beautiful, that creatures were made to live in harmony and peace, and that man was made for happiness and living on an intimate basis with God. But man sinned, and somehow the whole system that God had set up went awry. First, man experienced God's disappointment; then man found that he was no longer fit to live in paradise. Man had to work and struggle to live. Then brother turned against brother, and more sin, sorrow and pain filled the world. The Scriptures do not say it directly, but all lesser creation seems to be affected negatively by sin, too. Only after sin do the animals become wild and sometimes enemies to man. Only after sin are the ravages of nature mentioned.

Whether or not we take each word of the story of the fall literally, the *meaning* of the story is clear—sin disrupted all of creation, the way it was supposed to work together, and the beauty and pleasure that God had planned for man in it all. One of the prophesies of Isaiah, therefore, indicates that the Messiah, anointed with the Spirit, will restore all creation to its former peacefulness; animals will no longer find other animals to be enemies, and mankind will be at peace (Is 11:1-11). Thus, too, St. Paul in his Letter to the Romans (5:12-19) indicates that just as in Adam all men sinned and died, so also in Christ all men come into a new life. If the sin of Adam brought hostility, pain, suffering, and evil into the world, should not the saving work of Christ do more in the opposite direction?

Healing Brings Freedom

Jesus himself on several occasions indicated that the body and the "inner man" were so united that they affected each other intimately, with the result that sin leads to sickness and death, while his ministry of reconciliation leads to happiness and healing. The healing of the paralytic (Mt 9:1-8; Mk 2:1-12; Lk 5:17-26) indicates this truth clearly. A paralyzed man is brought to Jesus by friends who have faith that Jesus can heal him. (This detail about the friends' faith indicates to me the dynamics present in healing prayer: when I am sick and therefore weak in the faith in Jesus' love that is often needed for healing, I go to a friend who prays for me; Jesus sees *his* faith and heals me.) Jesus looks at the man and says, "Your sins are forgiven." Then he pronounces the man as whole—notice he does not pray a second time, for the forgiveness prayer seems to be enough for him—and tells the man to stand up. He is healed.

Freedom from sin and its effects brought health to that man's body, but Jesus healed the inner man first. He let him know that he was loved, that he was forgiven, that he no longer had to bear the guilt of his sin in his heart. He freed the man spiritually by forgiveness, emotionally by releasing him from the guilt that is sin's natural consequence, and intellectually by asserting the truth that sin does not have to rule the day. Then he proclaimed his body free, and it was.

In my own ministry I have seen the same thing happen

over and over again, sometimes quite dramatically. Maybe the story of which I am fondest is one that involves an infant, a little girl only nine months old. She had been born with severely dislocated hips, a congenital problem not too uncommon, mainly consisting in the fact that the hip socket and ball joint at the end of the femur were not entirely.formed. But this case was so acute that her doctor, one of the best specialists in the country, said that she probably would never walk, and if she did walk it would not be until her teenage years, and then only a little bit. In most cases this problem is not so severe and can be corrected with operations, casts, and braces for the first three to six years or so. But the future of this child was braces on her legs, casts, traction, operations, hospitals, and bone transplants, with little or no chance of her ever walking normally—in general a miserable childhood. When I met her she was in a cast from her waist down. Her parents had come to me, having just a few weeks before accepted the possibility that God might be able and willing to heal physical problems. Their faith was very tentative and their tendency to despair great. Their daughter was going into the hospital the following week for traction and a probable operation, and they asked me to pray for a complete physical healing.

Needless to say, interiorly I was not a little shocked by the size of their need which I felt even more intensely because of the desperation that filled them. I kept calm exteriorly, however, to encourage their faith—and mine—and told them that it seemed to me that all we need pray for was that God finish what he had started in the womb with this child, because for some reason her "creation" had been stopped before it was completed. Jesus loves little children so much and they are such open receptacles to his love because they have not personally sinned that I assured them that there should not be much problem in this at all.

But when I began to pray, another kind of intuition began to come over me; it prevented me from praying as I had planned, and, after a few minutes of silence, what came from my lips was a prayer for the inner being of this little girl. I prayed that Jesus would comfort her in all the pain she had felt in the womb—I saw her in my imagination there uncomfortable and confused because her body was not whole; in praying about her birth I almost felt with her the pain she must have endured as her hips, with no inner support or stability, were pressed and pushed by the contractions of her mother's body, and I asked Jesus to heal that pain. Then I began to feel the pain of living for this child, the pain that must have constantly filled her hips and legs for every moment of her life of nine months, and I asked Jesus to heal that.

Having united myself in this way with this child's world, I began to realize the frustration she endured all the nine months of her life by being in casts and traction, the frustration of motionlessness which for a baby must be great. I asked Jesus to come into that frustration and bring his peace and love to this little girl so that she would be confident deep within her that she was loved in a perfect and gentle way. Then we prayed about the future, that her hip sockets would be formed and that the ball joint at the end of the femur would be completed perfectly, and that her doctor would know just what to do to help this process along.

I finished the prayer and they left, not exactly sure of any real good coming to their daughter for their visit with me. I, too, if I am to be honest, must admit that I wondered as they left what exactly could or would be the outcome of such a seemingly hopeless situation. A few days later the father of the child came back to me and confirmed my worst fears as he said, "Well, your prayers didn't work. My daughter isn't any better at all. The doctor took X-rays of her legs this morning as she went into the hospital, and there is no change. Thanks for your time." Especially in that last "thanks for your time" I could hear the profound disappointment and alienation from God that he felt, and I felt powerless to do one thing about it. I felt so badly that when ten days later they tried to call me I did not return their call. I was afraid they were calling to blame me for the failure of healing in their daughter, and I felt I did not want to deal with those kinds of feelings.

But on the following Sunday I could not avoid them. They saw me out in front of church from afar and hailed me, then came quickly toward me. Both were talking to me at the same time. "Our daughter's leg is healed! One of her legs is healed!" It seems that following ten days of traction one hip socket and ball joint formed completely, and even the doctor said it was a miracle. Furthermore, the real miracle, as far as these two parents were concerned, was the change in attitude their daughter evidenced. From the day of the prayer she changed from a whining, complaining child to a content little girl. During her stay in the hospital she did not squirm and resist the rigidity of traction but rather remained still; and when her parents left the hospital to go home at night, she did not cry and carry on as she did during former hospital stays, but rather seemed content to be there. Even the nurses commented on how much improved her disposition was comparing these visits with previous ones. It was her mother's thought that she was content to be there because she was never alone; the look on her daughter's face seemed to assure her that Jesus was her constant companion, taking pain from her and bringing her peace.

It took one more year for the other hip socket to be healed, a wonderfully quick recovery in itself when we consider how severe her original problem was and how many years and operations the doctor had first projected for her. But now the healing is finished. This little girl is free from her limitation and is walking everywhere (and getting into a lot of trouble, too, just as a child her age should). She is free and whole after Jesus ministered to her, just as the paralyzed man in the Gospel story was. Free! Free from pain, guilt, illness, and evil, personal evil and/or the evil of the world.

Deep down inside, all of us want that kind of freedom. We want, and indeed—if we are going to be honest—need, freedom from so many things if our lives are going to be whole and happy and holy as we have intended them to be. If we have not already made a deal with life, compromised our goals so that they are now dim memories, or forgotten our dreams of whom we would become and what we could be, we are well aware that there is much need for freedom in our lives. Guilt strangles so many people, fear comes upon others to smother them, and still others fight pride from conquering their inner sense of value. Illness and pain follow many people around like a faithful but vicious pet. How much freedom we need when we look squarely at it! Maybe it is the size of our need that prevents us from looking hard. But in the depth of our hearts we know we are not meant to live bound in the chains of limitations, and we long to be free to be ourselves as we were created to be. We long for freedom, and yet we are afraid of it.

Afraid? Yes. Afraid because what is freedom but the unknown? Who knows what it is like to be free? And even if some people were to know, could they explain it so well that I could understand? Whether they know freedom or not, anyway, I do not know it—I do not feel free in the areas in which I need freedom. If I did know how it feels to be free, I would already be free. So freedom is an unknown to me—that is why I am afraid of it. Yet I know another feeling inside of me is just as true as my fear, and that is hurt—hurt that comes from the limitations that I feel. So I see that freedom from my limitations comes at a price: the pain of growing and the responsibility of being free. My healing unto freedom will not be a carefree road, but one of many troubles and much toil. The one difference—the one significant difference—however, between the troubles and toil I experience now and the troubles and toil on the road to freedom is that freedom's toil produces something valuable in the end, while today's toil gets me nothing. Also, I will not have to travel freedom's road alone.

But it is difficult to choose the hardship of transcending my present sad state; it is difficult to draw on the deeper and deeper parts of myself and to grow, change, and become a free creature. That is the reason that sometimes I choose quite clearly not to be free, in that I choose to sin. But then I usually know what I have done, that I have chosen a lesser road, a way of lighter cares, at least for the present, and so I feel guilty. When I find myself pushed and pulled by my awareness of my inner pain, my desire to be free of my pain, my fear of being free of my pain, my cowardice at sometimes choosing a lesser way, and my guilt over my cowardice, then I know one fact and I know it clearly—I have focused too much on *me*. My pain, my desire, my fear, my cowardice, and my guilt all are preventing me from looking to the wholeness that is at hand. They all prevent me from looking to the Lord, seeing the truth about me, and looking at the world from his point of view. Truly, at this point I need a Savior to pluck me free of the morass of my confused feelings. I need to see what God is doing now.

A lady who comes to our weekly parish prayer meetings has experienced this truth in a most clear way. Her list of problems would baffle the clearest of minds—her husband is emotionally unstable, one child was born with a physical handicap, another with a mental handicap, and a third has taken after his father in his illness. Consequently, this woman felt the responsibility of the whole family on her shoulders, and a heavy responsibility it was. Neighbors would find it difficult to talk with her because of her complaining; and also these pressures had taken a physical toll on her own body, so that she had suffered several heart attacks and other physical ailments. She was caught in her anger over her lot in life, her fear of what would happen next, her guilt over her lack of trust in God; and so she sank deeper and deeper into a world of rejection and pain. When the prayer meetings first opened she came to them tentatively, with an anxious faith (which was more like a desperate hope) that God would, that he *must*, do something. She attended the meetings once in a while for several months, mostly praying that God would give her the strength to live with all the members of her family who were in trouble. God usually gives us the spiritual gifts we ask for, so she did receive the strength she needed, but her situation did not change. Soon she began to sense that there was a greater power in prayer than she had ever realized, that God might have a different plan for her. She began to look at things from God's point of view and to see a hope. She began to sense that there were others who would reach out and help her, members of our prayer group and people all over the metropolitan area who were dedicated to using the power of prayer.

Finally she began to have faith that God loved her enough to heal her. Little by little this faith grew—first it was just a passing thought, a seed, then it blossomed as she saw and heard what God could do in the lives of others. Soon faith was more than just a part of her; it became *her* point of view. More and more she looked at her life and saw God doing good things for her and her family.

Finally, over a year after the day on which she had attended her first prayer meeting, she decided not to ask God for strength to live with her problems, but rather she asked him to heal her body. And it happened. "Ask, and it will be given to you," Jesus told us (Mt 7:7). Why should it surprise us that his word is true? From that day this woman has lived without pills and the other means she used to keep her sick body functioning, because her body is no longer sick. But since the rest of her family is still suffering she continues to pray, searching for a deeper faith in his love that heals while she continuously rejoices in what he has done.

God's Freedom Is Already Ours

Such things could be true for each of us. When we take our eyes off our own problems and we finally do look to the

Lord, we can hardly believe what he is doing. The promise and explanation of these wondrous truths are in his Bible—the word which tells us something that at first sounds almost ridiculous, except that he has said it. For he tells us that all the things we need, all the freedom that we seek—all the gifts of God—are ours, ours right now. We do not have to look around to find this freedom, we do not have to earn it in any way, nor do we have to convince God to give it to us. All we need do is let faith and love open our eyes—heal them of their spiritual blindness—to see that this freedom is and always has been before us. Whatever we need to save us from the evil of the world and its effects we have through the love of God. This plan for our salvation is revealed over and over again in God's word, e.g., in Paul's letter to the Ephesians (1:3-14), in which we learn that we can participate in the *full freedom of heaven*—which is wholeness—even while we live here on earth:

> Blessed be God the Father of our Lord Jesus Christ, who *has* blessed us with *all* the spiritual blessings of heaven in Christ. Before the world was made, he *chose us*, chose us in Christ, to be holy and spotless, and to live through love in his presence (Eph 1:2-4; italics mine).

Notice that Paul uses the past tense—all the blessings we can hope for are *already* ours. And not only has God already gifted us, but his decision to do so did not even happen "in time" but rather in eternity, "before the world was made." The fact that we are blessed with every spiritual blessing is a part of God's eternal plan, not an afterthought of his. What security this revelation gives to a believer! The statement Paul is making is reminiscent of Jesus' words, "I tell you therefore, everything you ask and pray for, believe that you have it already, and it will be yours" (Mk 11:24).

Furthermore, Paul says "he chose us." If he chose us

before the world began, that means he must have known us, loved us, singled us out, and made a plan for us. And what did he choose us for? "To be holy and spotless, and to live through love in his presence." Everything that a Christian hopes for all his life is contained in those words; indeed, a human being could not ask for more from God or anyone. He chose us "in Christ," Paul also notes. It is difficult for us to understand that in the one gift of Jesus to the world, God our Father gave us everything—everything we could need, want, dream of, hope for. His gift of Jesus to the world is so simple, so overwhelming in the statement of love that it makes, so complete, that mankind underestimates its significance. We constantly look for something more, but what could be more than that which we have in Christ?

Especially as we live each day, if we are aware of ourselves at all, we see so many needs and lacks within us, and we ask God to supply them, never considering the possibility—although he has said it in so many different ways—that he has already given us what we need. He has already declared where he stands and how he feels toward us; he has already made up his mind to give to us and he has informed us of his decision. What we need *is ours*, if we reach out to him in faith and say "Thank you." It is from this insight that Paul's letters are replete with the injunction to give thanks to God in all things and in all situations.

Paul continues:

[He chose us in Christ] determining that we should become his adopted sons, through Jesus Christ for his own kind purposes, to make us praise the glory of his grace, his free gift to us in the Beloved, in whom, through his blood, *we gain our freedom*, the forgiveness of our sins (Eph 1:4-7); italics mine).

The gifts we have been given, Paul says, are really one gift: although we do not deserve it, in Christ we have become "adopted sons" of the Father. No wonder God gives us so many blessings—we are part of the family. Any human parent who is a good person and who adopts a child into his family treats that child just as his own; indeed, the child *becomes* his very own child, first legally through the state, but even more important in his heart. If a human parent can adopt a child and treat him as his own, we cannot assume less for God. God's Son is Jesus Christ, and in our Father's eyes we are equal—not that we deserve it; rather it is "his free gift to us in the Beloved"—to Jesus. In other words, in whatever way the Father treats Jesus he will also treat us. His reason? "For his own kind purposes" is the reason Paul gives. To think that not only are we God's very own family, but that he has made us so out of the kindness of his heart, is a special thing. Surely, if we accept what God is saying through Paul and respond genuinely in our hearts, what he has done will "make us praise the glory of his grace." What a magnanimous gift! How incomparable a giver God is! Who could outdo him? We never could claim to be spiritual paupers or beggars, nor could we ever see ourselves as unloved or unlovable, if we would accept into the deepest parts of ourselves the truth of who we really are in God's eyes. And one of the aims and goals of God's healing power as it is released in our lives is just that— to help us accept, little by little, as we are able, his simple love.

But there is more! God seems to heap gift upon incredible gift. Not only are we each "his family" and cherished by him, but also through the gift of Jesus who died for us *"we gain our freedom."* He does not hold us bound so that we will always have to live under the onus of achieving or earning his love. Rather, once and for all he has declared us "forgiven" and "freed." We owe nothing, not even one little installment, on the price that was set for us. Maybe one of the reasons that people find this simple truth so difficult to accept without qualifying it is that this fact is based on the value of one life in whose shed blood *we find freedom*. And since we find it difficult to see the value in our own lives without qualifying our worth, it does not penetrate deeply into us that *one life* given humbly, simply, lovingly, could do all that God claims it has done. And so in our unacceptance and disbelief of God's word we continue to wait and ask for the salvation that is already ours, ready for us to take with a "thank you" said humbly, simply, and lovingly, in the very same way that the gift was given.

Such is the richness of the grace which he has showered on us in all wisdom and insight (Eph 1:8).

After receiving so much, to be told that God thought it would be *wise* for him to do all this for us is more than a person can bear. It was *wise* for God to love us and make us his children—that sounds as though he was doing himself a favor by saving us. And yet, is it not always that way with a real "giver"? One who gives with a truly generous heart, as God does, receives more than he gives.

He has let us know the mystery of his purpose, the hidden plan he so kindly made in Christ from the beginning to act upon when the times had run their course to the end: that he would bring everything together under Christ, as head, everything in the heavens and everything on earth. And it is in him that we were claimed as God's own, chosen from the beginning, under the predetermined plan of the one who guides all things as he decides by his own will; chosen to be, for his greater glory, the people who would put their hopes in Christ before he came (Eph 1:9-12).

In these words Paul tells us of the wonderful dignity that God has given to us; for not only has he loved and cherished, forgiven and freed us, but he also has shared openly his plan with us, "letting us in" on the inner meaning of the whole world. He has brought us to himself as his children and confidants, like a Father who shares with his child the management of his estate. He places great trust in us and puts great confidence in our abilities and in our loyalty to him. As he informs us that it is his will to "bring everything together under Christ," he gives to us who are the body of Christ in the world the task of participating in this great ministry of reconciling the world to the Father and bringing all creation under the aegis of his peace.

> Now you too, in him, have heard the message of the truth and the good news of your salvation, and have believed it; and you too have been stamped with the seal of the Holy Spirit of the promise, the pledge of our inheritance which brings freedom for those whom God has taken for his own, to make his glory praised (Eph 1:13-14).

In conclusion, then, Paul reminds us that not only the Jews, who first received the message of salvation, but also all the peoples of the world have heard "the message of the truth" and so can come to the Lord in faith. Because we are marked with "the seal of the Holy Spirit," we have received "the pledge of our inheritance which brings freedom" to us— freedom from every doubt or fear that our limitations will hold us back. After taking into our hearts the message of salvation as Paul explains it, we know that in the "real world"—the world of God's love—there is nothing that can hold us back. Nothing has that power unless I give it that power through sin or I am given into that power through the sin committed against me. In either of those situations God's healing power can reassert his place in my life as my Savior from everything that limits me.

It takes time and the right circumstances to let our hearts accept all the freedom that God wants to give us. When I first met my friend Nick, for example, he was a man who had made his way in the world by the sheer force of his own will. He was a good man with many decent values, but at this point in his life he was angry because his mother was dying. He asked me to visit her, and I did so the next day. That day, however, was the day of her death; I met Nick and his father in the hall of the hospital just outside her room, and I was able only to comfort them.

Nick was very bitter about his mother's death. Her life had been hard and her death early, and Nick blamed God. He was angry. Nick and I became friends, and soon I began to see the hardness in him mixed in with the goodness. Therefore I began to share with him about the Holy Spirit and what he could do to bring Nick into the "real world" of God's love. I gave him a book to read and it interested him. We talked occasionally for several weeks about spiritual matters, and finally he said that he wanted the power of the Spirit to be released in his life. And so we prayed and asked Jesus to do just that.

Nick's story is not a dramatic one, but rather a tale of gradual change and growth. He became more accepting and tolerant of ways other than his own. He began to see God working in his life and to forgive God for all the hurtful things in his life—especially his mother's death—for which he had held God responsible. Through faith and his new-found love of God he began to observe and confront his prejudices, his lack of trust, his pride, and his other sinful ways. His glory slowly became God alone and what *he* can do, whereas previously his glory had been Nick and what *he* could do.

All of this freedom came to Nick because through the enlightenment of the Holy Spirit he let Christ love him and gradually reveal to him all that was already his. He took on a positive attitude that God already has loved him so much that he has given him every good thing he will ever need. This attitude is what we call a practical day-to-day faith. It is a faith that God is not uninvolved but that he cares deeply. It is not the kind of faith that deals with abstract issues but rather one that says "God *loves . . . me . . . now!*" And so through this faith Nick made contact with God and invited him to take an ever more active role in his life. Then Jesus was free to heal Nick of the things in his life that made him hard, willful, and therefore bound up in loneliness. This kind of "healing" freed the inner man in Nick to be more alive, happier, and easier to get along with. No longer did he have the compulsive need to forge through life by the sheer force of his own will. As he relaxed to let God's will be done instead, he found that God's will was far more Leautiful for him than his own.

Nick's wife and children, family and friends will never tell anyone that Nick's life is perfect in any way—that would not be human. But he and all who know him will easily witness to the many changes that have caused the hardness in him to fall away, leaving a quiet, less boastful strength so that the innate goodness he always had is free to shine forth even more excitingly than ever. Nick says that the difference that he feels inside is like the one between night and day, between one side of the hand and the other.

Through Faith We Participate in Heaven

Jesus can heal the unfreedoms of Nick's or anyone's life because healing is the most real thing there is. Healing—the changes that come into our lives when God touches us—is not anything like magic or a fantasy. If anything is unreal—in the sense that it has no *real* power to destroy us in any ultimate way—it is the hurt, limitation, and evil that are of this passing world. One day all of those things will not exist at all, and so, in a sense, *they* are the fantasy. As Paul reminds us, one day not only will all evil pass away, but also everything except the love of God (1 Cor 13:8-10). The love of God has power over all things. And so God's love for me is the reason that he has already hidden my real self with Christ in God, and in the most real of ways the deepest and most important part of me, my spirit, already participates in heaven and its perfection (Col 3:3-4). In healing, Jesus merely reasserts the truth as he knows it and has won for us—that we are children of the Father, marked with the seal of the Holy Spirit, in whom we share in the promise God made to mankind. As children we have full rights of inheritance; and freedom—forgiveness, holiness, and healing—is our birthright in the Holy Spirit.

This birthright was given to us when we were baptized. In baptism we entered into the heavenly kingdom; baptism was our entrance rite into the freedom of God's kingdom. Through being born again of water and the Spirit we have been brought into a relationship with God by which we can call him *Abba*, an Aramaic diminutive of "Father" most properly translated as "Daddy." God is our Daddy because we have been born into his family, brothers and sisters of Jesus, co-inheritors of all that our Daddy has. Through our baptism we gain the right and privilege to be whole and holy, to be loved in an active way by God, to live with Jesus in the glory of his resurrection, to share in the full freedom that the Holy Spirit brings.

This simple but wondrous relationship with God is renewed when we are confirmed and when we are baptized in the Holy Spirit. God gives us a new experience of his love and power. He empowers us to be his *adult* children, responsible for a part of the kingdom, and he gives us the tools we need to accomplish our task, the gifts of the Holy Spirit.

The Eucharist also brings us into the heavenly kingdom a little bit more deeply each time we receive the sacred meal. The Eucharist, as is true of each of the sacraments, brings us into the heavenly kingdom in a different way or with a different emphasis. The eucharistic banquet is a foretaste of the full freedom of heaven, where we will know God directly and be filled entirely with him and with his love. Each time we receive Holy Communion we deepen the effect of his loving salvation in us. Through the bread and wine of Communion Christ becomes an actual part of us, working his way into the depths of the places within ourselves that have not yet accepted the freedom of wholeness. And as we accept wholeness in each part of our inner being, that part of us is healed from sin and its effects, and it feels a new freedom to be. As we proclaim in the Roman rite before receiving Communion, "Say but the word and I shall be healed."

Throughout his letters to the churches, Paul explains over and over again that because Christ has risen we also have risen to a new life; therefore we should live a new life, putting aside the bondage of all ways that are old and that keep us from believing that we are new. When I am filled with faith in the resurrected Lord, I live in such a way that is congruent with his teaching. When I forget that Jesus died and rose for me, and that consequently I am loved and redeemed—when I forget that I am free—I act accordingly, and that is when I sin. The experience of confessing one's sins, and in a special way the Roman rite of the sacrament of reconciliation, renews my freedom after these times when I forget that I am loved and redeemed at an exceedingly high price. At those times I need to know that the Lord understands my weakness, I need to be freed of my sin, I need to know that I am still loved although I have betrayed that love. The experience of reconciliation, then, brings me back into the kingdom when I have strayed from it, reminding me of who I am called to become. Thus it is a time of rejoicing and thanksgiving.

Similarly, I need to be freed and made whole when the evil of the world or the evil within me attacks me as an illness of a physical or psychological nature. Especially when I have been living my life for Christ and evil attacks as sickness, I need help, and anointing for healing—in the Roman rite the sacrament of anointing of the sick—is just the spiritual prescription that the Divine Physician ordered. "The prayer of faith will save the sick man and the Lord will raise him up again," said the apostle James in his Letter to all Christians (5:15). And it is true, because God has let us know that a Christian has the right to expect healing and wholeness for himself as a sign that he has entered already the heavenly kingdom. When sickness attacks, the sacrament of healing will bring us back into the full freedom of the kingdom of God.

Finally, the sacraments of marriage and holy orders empower people to bring this heavenly kingdom, this godly love and wholeness, into the world. These are the sacraments that give people special duties in the kingdom which bring it to greater fulfillment in the lives of all who have faith. People marked by these special encounters with the Lord bring his redemptive love into daily life in a unique way, by witnessing through the commitment of vows and promises to the Lord to his redemptive love here and now. In living his love in the midst of the strife of each day, they reveal the power that God's freedom has over the forces that are bent on destroying the goodness of our lives. These sacraments and the people who live them are signs to us of the strength God shows through human weakness.

The life of faith, then, and the life of the sacraments lead us into a new world of God's love. The faith that is God's gift to us and the intense encounters with Christ that we call sacraments bring us into an entirely new world that is fresh, exciting, good, and, what is best, holy. Because of God's love for us and his redeeming us we have been given a brand new life, an experience of the freedom of heaven within us. "The kingdom of God is close at hand," Jesus tells us. "Repent and believe the Good News" (Mt 1:15). "The experience of God's healing love is already within you," he is saying. "Repent." In other words, "Change your attitude, change your outlook; open your ears and eyes and minds, and comprehend what I am saying and all its implications for your life. Do not turn your back before you understand; listen, try again, and come to believe that what I say is true: you can come to know God personally as a friend and feel the good effects of his friendship in your life. This is no tired saying. It is news, Good News—for your lives can never be destroyed again once you believe and let me work the miracle of faith in you."

Because of God's participation in our life and ours in his, the most real way we can approach life is to say and believe that everything is new, especially us; that we are already participating in heaven because our spirits have been brought into that realm through faith and the sacraments; that we can see the effects of heavenly love—i.e., the freedom that is healing on the physical, emotional, intellectual, and spiritual levels—every day.

Often, however, we forget this point of view, we do not understand and yield to this freedom, and that state of being happens for many reasons. Maybe the pain of life confused us at so early an age that our eyes have been deflected from gazing at the truth. Maybe when we pray and ask God to show a bit of heaven right now in our lives our desire for immediate results prevents us from seeing the more gradual process of change and healing that God in his infinite wisdom has initiated. Maybe after we pray and things actually are changing in our lives we look within and see traces of former problems, and in our insecurity we judge that God has done nothing, while actually he has done much but not quite in the way we would have done it if we were in charge. Maybe our very desire to be in charge of our own lives prevents us from surrendering to God's authority through which we will find our only road to real freedom. Maybe we fall victim to that ever-present form of pride—demanding perfection from ourselves and judging ourselves—rather than accepting the fact that God is not finished molding us while we are still in this world.

Whether our reasons for not believing are these or one of

a host of others that are possible, we allow our human failings
to rob us of our faith, our direction, our hope, our perspective.
We begin to concentrate on ourselves altogether too much,
and inside in our aloneness is one place we will never find
freedom. When our attention is on ourselves in this way, it
cannot also be on the Lord. But with the Lord is where the
good things are happening. Where Jesus is present is where
healing will take place. Where God is present we cannot help
but find love and peace for ourselves.

These truths were never more dramatically known by me
than when I met a woman in October 1975 who was to lead
me into the most remarkable example of physical healing I
have ever experienced. This woman asked me to pray with her
because she believed that Jesus wanted to heal her deafness,
and all the circumstances in her life led to me as the one who
would be the channel of his power.

This woman's hearing had been tested many times as
approximately seventy-five percent deficient. She could hear
the spoken voice if it were louder than a conversational tone,
but she could not hear soft voices, background noises, nuances
of music or other such sounds. The doctors had concluded
after years of testing and operations on her inner ear that the
damage must be in the nerve that connected the ear to the
brain. They assumed that this damage could have been
brought about by one or both of two circumstances of her life:
a fall from a horse and minor concussion that was not medi-
cally treated at the time of the accident almost fifteen years
before, and the eight years that this woman spent as a vocalist
for rock bands with their extremely loud music attacking her
ears night after night. It was after her last unsuccessful operation that even the doctor said that all she could do now was to
pray.

Of course, she took his statement as a sign of the complete
hopelessness of the situation until she was led through renewed faith to seek spiritual help. She attended the large meet-

ing of a well-known faith healer, and while nothing happened at the time she felt assured in her heart that this was the road she should pursue and that the solution to her problem would come soon. She heard about Father Francis MacNutt and his tremendous healing ministry, and so she wrote to him for advice and/or an appointment to see him. He wrote back to her that she was welcome to come to see him in St. Louis, Missouri, but that I lived right in her own area and that I could probably help her. She conferred with a mutual friend of ours and found it was true that I prayed for healing, and so she called and asked for my assistance. She told me that she had great faith that Jesus would restore her hearing through prayer and that God wanted to use me for that prayer.

I remember quite clearly the day I went to see her and the visit we had. We gathered with two friends of hers and prayed. I stood behind her and placed my hands on her head and ears, asking God to restore the nerves that controlled hearing and any part of the hearing mechanism that had been traumatized in any way. Her prayer was a simple one, focusing on Jesus' love. We prayed for a short period of time, five or ten minutes. When I finished praying I walked from behind her around to the front so that I could speak to her, but before I could say a word she said, "What's that!" I stopped, puzzled by her comment, when one of her friends noticed that as I walked around her a floorboard had creaked. Then she said, "I can hear the children playing. How far away are they?" One of the others looked out the window and said they were down the street.

She became very intense and then said, "That was a bus that just went by." We confirmed that she was correct, but then she commented, "But there's no bus that passes along this street."

That was when I realized what God had done, and I said, "You're right. That bus was on Austin Boulevard, two blocks away."

A year later I called her to find out how she was and especially how her hearing was progressing. She told me that her hearing level had maintained the top level it achieved on the day of our prayer. She said that she had gone back to the doctor for his opinion, and he confessed that he could not explain the dramatic recovery in any medical way; and when he tested her hearing he found it to be perfectly normal. By centering on what Jesus could do for her through faith she was healed.

While the healing of this woman's hearing was instantaneous on the day of the prayer and, in that sense, might be called a "miracle," in actuality there was nothing instantaneous about it at all. For several months the Lord had been leading her into the situation whereby he would bring new life into her hearing. Step by step he had deepened her faith in him, led her to trust him, and taught her many other spiritual truths not recorded here. She had been on a long journey with God before her hearing was restored, and she had continued on her journey with him as she allowed him to do many other things to change her life. Truly, this healing was one of many steps that God used to bring her close to him in his kingdom. It was through this healing that her faith was confirmed—her faith that God had already made her new—and the prayer we prayed together helped to reveal the truth of the "real world" of God's love, i.e., the truth of the kingdom that she was free from all limitation.

We come to understand, then, that we must look at things from God's point of view to develop a proper perspective. When our attention is on Jesus and what he is doing, our spirits are stimulated to remember what he has already done for us, that he has already not only brought us into the kingdom but also through the experiences of the sacraments let us taste the new wine of freedom, love, and peace. With our eyes on our Savior, our spirits remember what has happened to us and who we really are in God's eyes.

This is the very reason that Paul instructs Christians in his letters to praise God always, to pray unceasingly, and even to live a moral life; for in doing these things we are forced to remember. We are keeping our eyes—indeed, our lives—focused on Jesus who is loving, redeeming, and healing us. This is the way that we begin to live in the world of God's wholeness, the kingdom of heaven. For when we are united with Jesus by keeping our attention on him, our spirits remember what they really are, that they first of all belong to no one else but God, that in his hands they have become whole (and they are the very center of who we are as human beings), and that they are lovable. Maybe the last is the most difficult truth that God calls any of us to believe during our lives.

Jesus' Parables of Great Assurance

For most people, it seems, the great issue of their faith life is not whether they believe in the resurrection of Jesus or in the Trinity or anything like that. These are matters to which we easily give our assent. What is difficult for most of us to believe, because it involves our emotions, our past experience, and our attitudes about life as well as our intellects and spirits, is that God cares about each of us—now! In teaching this unfathomable truth Jesus used the simplest of metaphors in two parables that scholars have named the Parables of Great Assurance. Each parable is only one or two verses long, and just in that quality of brevity they stand out.

He put another parable before them, "The kingdom of heaven is like a mustard seed which a man took and sowed in his field. It is the smallest of all the seeds, but when it has grown it is the biggest shrub of all and becomes a tree so that the birds of the air come and shelter in its branches." He told them another parable, "The kingdom of heaven is like the yeast a woman took and mixed in with three measures of flour till it was leavened all through" (Mt 13:31-33).

Living in the kingdom of heaven is the topic of this entire chapter; all the references to the heavenly state our spirits live in have shown that the kingdom becomes real to us because of God's love of us and our faith in him. Living in the kingdom is another way of talking about the redeemed spirit living in the loving presence of Jesus; it is another way of talking about Jesus' presence with each baptized, believing Christian. When the parables begin with, "The kingdom of heaven is like. . . ." we can read, "The presence of Jesus within us is like. . . ."

First, it is like a mustard seed that grows and grows until it becomes a huge shrub in which birds can find some rest. In other words, Jesus' presence within us is at first like a small seed; but inevitably the seed germinates and grows, a little at a time, until it becomes big and something quite different from a seed. Can we stop a seed from growing? Can we stop Jesus from becoming more and more a part of our lives? Can we stop the kingdom from overtaking us? No! Just as inevitably as the seed that must grow unless something radical is done to it, so also will Jesus grow within us. He will overtake our whole beings and make us something quite different from what we are now. Before the mustard tree grew there was nothing in the place it came to occupy. That place was empty and dead. So too we are empty and dead until Jesus comes into us and begins to grow. But once he begins his work in us, he takes on his own momentum; we are able to slow him down by not giving him the best of conditions in which to grow, but it would be difficult to stop him altogether. As he reaches maturity in us—or as we reach maturity in him—we become something like a tree, strong, beautiful, vibrantly alive, and a haven for those who are weaker than ourselves. And his promise is that this state *will* come to be.

Similarly, Jesus said that he acts like yeast inside of us. Once the yeast is in the flour nothing can take it out again, and very little can prevent it from having its effect. The mixing will take a little time and so will the rising of the dough, but inevitably it will become ready for baking. Once Jesus comes into our hearts through faith he begins *his* process of transformation in us. Like yeast, he disappears and spreads throughout our entire beings, making our lives what they should be. The sacraments and other experiences of faith we have provide the right conditions for this transformation.

Some people think that it is easy to lose the presence of Jesus within them. These parables offer us the great assurance that nothing could be further from the truth for one who has truly invited him into his life at one point or another. From that point on Jesus is firmly planted, rooted, and growing. In growing he changes our lives, and that process of changing we call healing.

Real healing, then, is God acting in my life, making it "abundant," freeing me, making me whole. This is something that is always happening if I have invited God to live with me. How to pray for special healing—in other words, how to capitalize on God's blessings for me and use them to greater effect in changing my life—is a subject we all can learn much about because it means being in a simple, loving, faith-filled relationship with God.

But what does *not* happen in our lives is a series of "healings," in the sense of God starting and stopping action that will free us and change us. God does not hop in and out of our lives; rather, as Jesus has assured us he is always there, loving us in the best possible way at any given moment. The transformation and healing that we experience are not separate actions of God for us, done to reward us for being good, but they are different manifestations of his one act of love. For the freedom that comes from healing is a process, and, as is true of anything that God does, it happens in history, for history is God's workshop. What is history but a series of minutes and days, months and years, centuries and eons, filled with the experiences of mankind and all creatures? History is time, and time also is God's creature. He uses time, works in time to effect his will. Although he himself is timeless, he does not disregard time and history and interfere in the world. On the contrary, he is already in the world, around the world, within every creature of the world, including time, in order to bring each to its fulfillment in love. As the Lord of time and the Lord of life, he is also the Lord of *my* time and of *my* life, the number of years and of experiences that I call my own personal history.

The moments of extraordinary change and healing that we experience, then, are like windows through which we see into the spiritual world or the kingdom of heaven to the way things *really are* deep within creation and the way they will all appear to be in completion on the day when the whole world sees him face to face. We can be assured that God continues to work lovingly for us, just as we can be assured that a tree will continue to grow and that yeast will continue to leaven. The transformation that God works continuously in us, the healing unto abundant life that is a *normal* manifestation of his presence within us with each experience, takes on a wider and wider effect in our lives, a deeper and deeper meaning for us. Our whole lives come under the gentleness of his strength and the freedom that only his love can bring. That limitless love is the reason that anyone who has come to know him in a personal way wants to praise him and thank him always.

Chapter III

What Is the Prayer of Loving Faith?

The kind of prayer that is used in the ministry of healing is called the prayer of faith. The name is somewhat of an anomaly, for what should prayer be, any kind of prayer, if not an expression of faith. Yet many prayers we pray are really prayers of non-faith—they are prayers of anxiety, prayers of anguish, prayers of despair. We pray many kinds of prayer that do not express our trust in the power and love of God to give us an abundant life, and so these prayers lack power. They do not accomplish what we need; they do not bring about the results we seek and God wants. So many Christians are caught in a morass of confused words aimed at what they think is an ambivalent or capricious God who sometimes even visits evil on us—"for our own good," of course—that they finally drop the whole endeavor of prayer, quite logically with these attitudes, as useless.

Although traditionally this prayer has been called the prayer of faith, I have chosen for my own use to rename it the "prayer of *loving* faith," because it seems to me that love is as essential as faith in this kind of praying. Love is the best motive for praying, but even more importantly love is Jesus' motive for acting when we pray to him. When we unite ourselves with his loving mind and heart we open up a new power to our prayer.

Faith without love, it seems to me, is a very dangerous

59

thing. Faith without love can seem to manipulate the people for whom we pray, or even to manipulate God. If I prayed for a person without loving him, I might pray that he become what *I* think he should be instead of praying for God's abundant life to be revealed in him; and if I prayed to God without loving *him*, I would end up asking for what *I* wanted, when *I* wanted it, *just because* I wanted it. And it is good to emphasize the love that is needed in praying for healing because it takes the focus off the minister of healing and redirects it to the needs of the person who seeks help and to Jesus, whose concern for this person is the source of all healing power.

When we pray for healing our faith needs to be "loving" so as to bring Jesus—who is all love—to the person who needs him to heal him. And our faith needs to be "loving" also in the sense that the minister of healing must, just as Jesus always did in the Gospel stories, never condescend to the person to whom he ministers, or be rough or crude with him, or make him feel guilty for his problem, or hurt him in any way. It is Jesus' love that will heal a person, and that love is often brought to that person through the love and faith of another.

And so prayer must come from faith and trust and love to succeed; when there is faith, trust, and love in prayer it *will* succeed. And why should not our prayers succeed? "Ask, and it will be given to you," the Lord said (Mt 7:7). What, then, is in our way? Why are our prayers not successful? Why do they come from anxiety and lead to more anxiety? "I don't know if the Lord wants me well," we say, or "If it's the Lord's will my problems will be solved," or, maybe most destructively of all, we might say, "This is my cross to bear in life; I must be happy because the Lord lets me share his sufferings through my illness." Of course, as Dennis and Matt Linn point out in their wonderful book *Healing of Memories* (Paulist Press, 1975), there are those rare people whose illness turns them outward toward others to help them, and these God usually will not heal. The type of person I refer to here is not this type, but rather the person whose illness is doing no good yet does not believe God wants him well.

Healing itself is nothing but answered prayer or "successful" prayer. From that point of view, there is nothing extraordinary about it at all, for why should we not expect God to answer our prayers after he has promised to and told us he would be delighted to give us an abundant life? If we did not expect God to answer our prayers we would have no reason to pray at all. On the subject of prayer Christians have been, it seems, quite double-minded and confused. Either it is worthwhile to take the time and effort to talk to our God and relate to him by telling him what we need—worthwhile because we know he will hear us and respond to our words—or it is not. If it is not, we should give up all prayer of petition immediately. If, on the other hand, it is worthwhile, we should be expecting things to happen as a result of our prayers, without any "ifs," "buts" or "maybes" qualifying our expectations. But even not all healing prayers are totally successful, and there are many reasons for that part of the Christian experience which the great evangelists and teachers of healing have listed in their works. One reason is that "healing" and "prayer" are both gifts of the Holy Spirit, and like any gift they need to be developed and used under God's direction. The extent to which a gift is developed is the extent to which it will be able to be used successfully.

Who Can Pray for Healing?

A truth that surprises many Christians when they first hear it is that each of us has the gifts of healing and prayer right now. Yes, it is true. Each of us has all the gifts of the Holy Spirit (enumerated by St. Paul in 1 Corinthians 12:4-11) and have had them since we were baptized. The gifts of the

Spirit are our birthright as children of God, our inheritance from the Father. When we were baptized the Holy Spirit came to live in us and make us his "temples," and with him he brought all of his gifts, which are really different aspects of himself or different ways he manifests himself in our lives. The Holy Spirit, as one of the three Persons of the Trinity, is divinely simple—he is infinite and indivisible. He cannot give part of himself, for he is not in parts. Therefore when he comes to a person in baptism he brings all of himself and all of his gifts, including the gifts of prayer and healing.

Why, then, do we not pray for healing? When I first faced that question, it was the various healing texts in the Bible that helped me most to find my way, especially those parts of the Gospels where Jesus sent his disciples out to preach the Good News. These became interesting to me because of their quiet insistence that healing could happen wherever the Gospel is preached.

For example, in the tenth chapter of his Gospel account, Matthew has Jesus instructing the apostles how to preach the Gospel and warning them of the problems they can expect along the way. The first thing Jesus does is to give them "authority over unclean spirits with power to cast them out and to cure all kinds of diseases and sickness" (Mt 10:1). And a little later he instructs them: "And as you go, proclaim that the kingdom of heaven is close at hand. Cure the sick, raise the dead, cleanse the lepers, cast out devils" (Mt 10:6-8). Jesus prepared the twelve for preaching by empowering them with his own power and expecting them to use it to heal all who were ill. Preaching and healing are mentioned in the same breath to instruct the apostles in their mission and duty. But that was just for the apostles, we may say, for Jesus was speaking to them as the kingdom was just being established.

But then we turn to the tenth chapter in Luke's account; this scene is taking place after the apostles have been sent forth and returned and Jesus is sending out the seventy-two disciples two-by-two, and as he instructs these disciples we hear him give a similar command: "Whenever you go into a town . . . cure those in it who are sick, and say, 'The kingdom of God is very near to you' " (Lk 10:8-9). The implication in this teaching is too clear to overlook: that they will know that the kingdom is near *because* they have seen the healing power of God. And the seventy-two come back rejoicing that they experienced all of Jesus' power in their ministries. Now, the apostles were important men, and we can expect them to be healers and miracle-workers, but the seventy-two were not so very important; after all, we do not even know their names. Yet Jesus empowered them, commissioned them, and expected them to heal and preach. But, we can still say, that was just for those few men who helped Jesus establish the kingdom.

Finally, however, we turn to the sixteenth chapter in Mark's Gospel where Jesus is giving his last instruction before he ascends to his Father. Some wonder whether we can say with any justification that these are the words of Jesus. The Scripture scholars tell us that the original ending to Mark's Gospel was lost and this one was added on years later. Whether or not these are Jesus' exact words, however, these instructions do proclaim the faith of the early Christian community as founded by the apostles on the faith of the apostles. These words indicate to us the common belief of the early Church and as such would, at the very least, be based on experiences to which they could personally testify. And this is what we read: "These are the signs that will be associated with believers"—notice the text does not say apostles or disciples or the seventy-two, but rather *all* who believe in Jesus—"in my name they will cast out devils; they will have the gift of tongues; they will pick up snakes in their hands, and be unharmed should they drink deadly poison; they will lay their hands on the sick, who will recover" (Mk 16:17-18). The meaning of the text as it stands is unmistakable. All who believe will be able to heal. That means that anyone who ever lives and has the chance to believe can share Jesus' ministry of healing. Jesus indeed expects his believers to be able to heal in his name. Parenthetically, we might add that the words about snakes and poison do not, as some claim, tell us to handle serpents or drink poison as a proof of Jesus' life within, but rather say that should these things inadvertently happen to a believer he will be protected.

There are many corroborating texts in the Gospels urging us to pray for healing, for abundant life. And many other texts in the Scriptures only begin to yield their fullest meaning when understood in terms of this expectation of Jesus that his believers would heal. For example, "Stay in the city, then, until you are clothed with the power from on high" (Lk 24:29). The power for what?—to establish the kingdom by preaching and healing. "If you remain in me and my words remain in you, you may ask what you will and you shall get it" (Jn 15:7). Ask for what?—anything, including that people be healed. "I tell you most solemnly, whoever believes in me will perform the same works as I do myself, and he will perform even greater works, because I am going to the Father" (Jn 14:12). The term "works" in the Gospel of John refers specifically to Jesus' miracles and healings.

The evidence in the Gospels pointing to healing as an essential activity for Christians is overwhelming. Jesus linked the preaching commission of the apostles, disciples, and all believers to a commission to heal as well. Healing was to be the visible sign that the Good News of peace, reconciliation, and God's loving care of man was now the law of the kingdom. This Good News is God's word which he will not allow to come back to him void, but rather it must accomplish what it says. And the accomplishment of the word is called healing—wholeness restored to a broken world, and freedom to every creature in that world who has been destroyed, limited, or hurt in any way by sin and its effects. In other words, abundant life is ours.

The full force of this way of understanding the ministry of Jesus and his Church cannot be seen until we look at the record that we possess of how the early Christians lived this new life in Christ, this Good News which he spoke through his life, death, and resurrection. The record I am referring to is the Acts of the Apostles. This book tells us what the early Church did with the new power unleashed in the world by Christ. Specifically, we can look in this work for the results of Jesus' commission to the disciples to heal, and for any indications contained in the book as to how important healing was in the early Church.

First of all, it is interesting to point out that the title of the book in the original Greek is not the Acts of the Apostles. In Greek the title reads *Praxeis Apostollon*, or "Acts of Apostles." The Greek article *ho* ("the") is conspicuously absent. Another way of translating the title is "What Apostles Did" or "What Apostles Do." Whoever attached this title to the work seems to be indicating that, at least devotionally, this book can be read as a personal instruction for Christians in how we are to be apostles for Christ.

There are many healing accounts in Acts, and they seem to be divided into three categories. There is something unique we can learn from each kind of story. The first kind involves the stories of healings that lead to persecution. The story of Peter and John healing the paralytic at the Beautiful Gate (Acts 3:1—4:31) is a prime example. After Peter and John heal the man in the name of Jesus of Nazareth, they are led before the Sanhedrin and told not to preach or heal in the name of Jesus.

When the apostles went back to the community they faced a choice: they could obey the Sanhedrin and stay out of trouble, or they could continue preaching and healing and risk their safety, their security, and their very lives. If healing had not been important to them, if Jesus had given the apostles the slightest indication that he did not command them to heal, that it was not essential to the preaching of the Gospel, it would seem logical that this would be the time for the Christians in Jerusalem to cease the practice of healing in favor of other methods of spreading the faith—methods not so irritating to the authorities. It is under persecution that movements are stripped to their barest essentials, and for quite logical reasons. But notice what the apostles do. They return and pray, "And now, Lord, take note of their threats and help your servants to proclaim your message with all boldness, *by stretching out your hand to heal and to work miracles and marvels* through the name of your holy servant Jesus" (Acts 4:29-30; italics mine).

There are two things to note. First, the community prays for more, not less, power to heal to be shown in their midst. These miracles will finally lead to the arrest of the apostles. The Church's defiance of the Sanhedrin's order indicates the importance, indeed the centrality of healing for the apostles in the Good News as they received it from Jesus himself. If healing is important enough to be persecuted for it, to be jailed for it, and to die for it, the implication is strong that it is indispensable. Secondly, the apostles' prayer is for the Lord's assistance so that they will preach *by* healing and miracle-working. This is no implication but a statement of faith. Preaching the Good News in the apostles' eyes *meant* healing in Jesus' name. They could not imagine preaching the Gospel of abundant life, reconciliation, and love without showing that it *happens now* through faith in Jesus. The God whom the apostles preached was a God who had power to change things for the better now; that is how he loves.

A second account of healing that led to persecution is the story of Stephen (Acts 6:8—8:3). The story begins with the statement that "Stephen was filled with grace and power and *began to work miracles and great signs* among the people" (Acts 6:8; italics mine). Words like "great signs" and "wonders" were Old Testament jargon for healings and miracles. Stephen was a healer like the apostles and his power was attracting many people to the faith. So hecklers came forward to engage him in debate, and because of what he said, not only was he killed but also a great persecution of the Church began (Acts 8:1). Still the preaching through healing did not stop; immediately Acts records that Philip is preaching and healing in Samaria and converting many to the way (Acts 8:4-8). From stories like these we can conclude that healing was an intrinsic part of the message, and the apostles were willing to endure and lead the whole Church if necessary into persecution, suffering, and even death because of the way of Jesus which included the practice of healing.

The second type of healing account in the Book of Acts is the healing of multitudes. Of this type there are many examples: all the apostles worked miracles by the laying on of hands, and people even waited for Peter's shadow to fall on their sick friends expecting healing (Acts 5:12-16); Philip was respected in Samaria for all the miracles he had done as well as for the ones the people saw with their own eyes (Acts 8:4-8); Paul and Barnabas performed signs and wonders by the grace of God in Iconium (Acts 14:3); Paul's reputation for healing was so widespread and powerful that his handkerchiefs and articles of clothing were taken to the sick who were healed (Acts 19:11-12). One of the points these stories make is that healing and miracles were common.

In our day, if we were writing about miracles that happened to people we knew or through someone we knew, we would probably be anxious to give names, dates, and circumstances in detail, all to lend credibility to what we were saying. We would do that because healings are uncommon in our experience, or at least in the experience of the people for whom we would be writing. But apparently healings and miracles were so common in apostolic times that the writer of Acts did not feel it necessary—indeed, probably found it impossible—to give the details of all the healings. Why were miracles so common then? Maybe the reason was that the members of the early Christian community took Jesus literally when he said he empowered, commissioned, and expected them to pray for healing in his name. Jesus honored their faith with wondrous results.

The third type of healing account in the Book of Acts involves individual healing stories, including even raisings from the dead; there are two, possibly three of these stories, depending on how the details of one of them are interpreted. In chapter nine Peter raises a holy woman, Dorcas, from the dead (vv. 36-43); later Paul is stoned and "left for dead" (this is the story open to different explanations) but was raised to immediate health by the prayers of his friends (Acts 14:19-20); and in Troas while Paul was preaching at a late-evening Eucharist a boy who was sitting on a windowsill became drowsy and fell three stories to the ground, but Paul's prayers saved him (Acts 20:7-12). Other healing accounts from different diseases and problems are too numerous to describe here. We can learn from them the fact that the Lord has power to bring wholeness to every kind of situation that is limiting to man, including death. We can also see that these healings were performed "in the name of Jesus Christ," and that many of the first Christians had the faith to accomplish great things in Jesus' power and love.

For it was not the apostles or disciples who healed any of these people, but rather Jesus working through them. That is the reason that we can even hope to see healing in the Lord's name today. The apostles have died and their particular gifts are gone from this earth, but Jesus still lives in his people, caring for them in his eternally loving way. "And know I am with you always; yes, to the end of time" (Mt 28:20). His promises still challenge us and ring in our ears: "Whatever you ask for in my name I will do, so that the Father may be glorified in the Son. If you ask for anything in my name, I will do it" (Jn 14:13-14). Jesus loves his people, and his desire is to take care of all of us, but he seems to be relying on us to have faith enough to ask and expect him to heal.

All of us, then, must look at ourselves—since we are accountable for our gifts as Jesus told us in the parable of the talents—and ask ourselves why we cannot pray for healing with success. Any gift that God gives us must be developed; God does his giving that way to give us a sense of dignity and worth, for we would not think much of ourselves if God did everything for us. One reason most Christians could list for their lack of "success" in "answered prayer" or healing is that they have not developed their gift—they did not know they had it, or they did not know it could and should be developed, or they did not know *how* it can be developed.

We know we have the gift of healing and we know it must be developed, so let us find out how to develop it. In a surprisingly short passage of Scripture, Jesus gives his apostles the basic rules to develop their gift and pray the prayer of loving faith. Jesus and the apostles had just entered Jerusalem for the final act in the drama of Jesus' ministry, and during this time they walked from Jerusalem to Bethany several times— perhaps to visit friends in Bethany. Whatever the reason for the walks, one day Jesus passed a fig tree, and when he wanted some of the fruit of the tree but found none, he cursed the tree. The next day as they passed by the tree again, they saw the fig tree withered to the roots.

> Peter remembered. "Look, Rabbi," he said to Jesus, "the fig tree you cursed has withered away." Jesus answered, "Have faith in God. I tell you solemnly, if anyone says to this mountain, 'Get up and throw yourself into the sea,' with no hesitation in his heart but believing that what he says will happen, it will be done for him. I tell you therefore: everything you ask and pray for, believe that you have it already, and it will be yours. And when you stand

in prayer, forgive whatever you have against anybody, so that your Father in heaven may forgive your failings too" (Mk 11:20-25).

Parenthetically, I find it interesting that Jesus uses the example of a withered fig tree to teach about how to have prayers answered. He had done many great works and healed people of incurable diseases and possesion, but he had not used those occasions to teach his disciples "how to do it." Maybe he taught them on this occasion because at those other times the apostles were so awestruck at the miracles he had just performed they were not open to being taught. Also, at those times there often were large crowds around the scene, and I can imagine so many people, not wanting to bother the Master himself or feeling unable to get his attention, asking the apostles all kinds of questions; and, humanly speaking, I can also imagine the apostles feeling so important because they were friends of Jesus that they were not ready to be taught at that time. It seems to me to be characteristic of Jesus, as a good teacher, to choose an example without any built-in distractions to teach his friends the important lesson of how to minister the gift of healing through prayer.

In these six verses, then, Jesus outlines the essential elements of a healing prayer, and he teaches four simple lessons: trust, take dominion over creation, claim your (Jesus') request, and forgive.

Trust

First, Jesus tells us to trust: "Have faith in God." It is a simple statement, but profound, for we are so willing to have faith in our own abilities, as far as they will take us, and we are so able to trust the forces of the world that we can understand to act predictably for us, but how difficult it is for us to trust our unseen God—to trust that he will be good to us. Yet, how many times did Jesus assure us that God is our Father, that he cares for us? Think of your own fathers, he said. Would they ever do anything on purpose to hurt you? Would they give you a stone to eat if you were hungry or put a poisonous snake in your hand if you asked for some fish? Of course not (cf. Lk 11:11-12), but we suspect God of doing those things; we find it difficult when we are hurting to go to him, confidently expecting him to understand and give us what we need. Jesus' logic on this point convicts us of our lack of trust: "If you then, who are evil, know how to give your children what is good, how much more will the heavenly Father give the Holy Spirit to those who ask him?" (Lk 11:13).

God is trustworthy; we can talk to him and know he will not laugh in our faces or turn away from us. When we go to him and ask for healing, he wants the person or situation we are praying for to be whole more than we want to ask him for it. He is our Father, loving and caring, so Jesus is right in telling us to begin by trusting him. If we find we cannot trust him, maybe it is because we cannot trust ourselves or others. If we cannot trust God it is not because he is untrustworthy, or because we cannot be sure he is on our side, but because we have learned a habit of cynicism and doubt. Since he is our Father, Jesus says, we know he wants everything good for us. His general will is that each of his children be happy, healthy, whole and holy.

So when we pray we can pray positively. We do not have to change his mind, for he is already on our side—he already wants what we want when it is good for us. And we do not have to rant and rave in our prayer as we so often find ourselves doing. Underneath our ranting and raving are two implicit attitudes: that God will not help us unless we prove to him that we deserve his help, and that God is not easily convinced.

Trust, simple and childlike—how important it is! And

how elusive! Yet, as we develop our trust in God, as we confront our mixed attitudes and confused feelings, as we allow the simplicity of Jesus' truth to calm the complex and raging emotions within, we must also be realistic about the depth of trust we have at any given moment. If we have learned to be afraid that God really does not love us, that fear will not disappear overnight nor will it disappear after one successful healing prayer. We must always be careful not to pray for things our faith will not encompass, so as not to be disappointed again and lose heart or to disappoint others. Faith—trust in God—is our first link to his healing love released in our lives, so we must nurture it carefully. Each time a need is before me I therefore ask myself, "Can my faith be stretched to being confident that God will do *even that* for me?" For if in my heart of hearts I did not believe God wanted to heal my sore throat yesterday, and so it still hurts, how can I believe he will heal my broken arm today? Trust, real and simple, is our first step to effective prayer.

Maybe it is easiest to see the effectiveness of simple trust in the lives of children. If we watched and listened closely to the children around us, most of us could relearn many of the simple truths of life. There is a little boy in my parish who is one of the best ministers of healing I know. He has listened to his Daddy and to me praying for healing and quickly has learned how to do the same. With a childlike trust in his own father, whose example he imitates, but also with a simple trust in Jesus because he knows that Jesus is good, this lad of six prays for anyone in the house who is sick. Mother, father, brother, and sisters—all have been delivered from much pain through his uncomplicated trusting prayers: "Jesus, Daddy doesn't feel good. Make him feel better. Amen." That is about all he says but he believes and he loves his family. God honors that kind of prayer. As we learn to be that uncomplicated and trusting, maybe our prayers will become as effective as his. The security of our Father's love will enfold us again, and we will understand with trusting hearts what our sophisticated minds could never grasp.

Sharing the Authority of Jesus

The second step Jesus gives his disciples is to take dominion over creation: "I tell you solemnly, if anyone says to this mountain, 'Get up and throw yourself into the sea. . . .' " The simple truth is that we have the power to command creation. This power comes to us through Jesus: "All authority in heaven and on earth has been given to me" (Mt 28:18). And Jesus chooses to share it with us who believe in him, for he commissions us to act in his name and spread the Good News to all creation.

The fact that the Christian has authority over creation may seem unusual to anyone who has lived his life presuming that the "laws of nature" were untouchable and immutable. With their thinking based on this presumption, most people have not experienced sharing in Jesus' power to change things from what they are to what they should be. Yet it is ours to share in faith and love, for Jesus needs people to act in his name, to continue to speak to creation broken by sin and urge it lovingly to function properly again. This is part of Jesus' healing mission on earth and so it is part of the mission of the people in whom Jesus lives.

God created the world perfect and he intends that it function as perfectly as possible. As we use his authority, God only asks that we remember that it is *his* authority, and that we ask his permission and find out if it is part of his loving plan in this particular situation to change things. By seeking God's guidance and acknowledging his supreme authority we become obedient servants performing God's work in the world.

I was surprised myself to learn how literally this was true when in 1974 I heard Agnes Sanford tell several of her experiences of commanding creation. She spoke of a time when she was flying over one of the western states and she happened to look down and see a house on fire. Immediately she asked God's permission, and when she felt that "go ahead" spiritual feeling that people who work closely with God quickly learn to discern, she spoke a word of command to the fire as a creature of God that it should abate. Quite soon the fire lost its power and disappeared.

Another time she reported being in her home state of California at a speaking engagement while one of the tremendous forest fires that that section of the country experiences was destroying woods, animals, and finally homes over a lengthy period of time. When she found time to pray about it she went down to the seashore so as to be in God's quiet and asked God if he wanted her to pray and how. Soon she received a gentle inspiration to pray for a change of wind from westerly to easterly, bringing with it the dampness of the sea while also stopping the westward surge of the fire. By the next morning all of God's creatures had obeyed her command because it was also Jesus' loving command, and the fire ceased to destroy.

It shows how well Christians understand this concept of our power to command creation that even the faith-filled audience listening to Mrs. Sanford laughed nervously at these witness stories. Why, however, should it not be true? God made human beings at the pinnacle of his creation in his own image and likeness. Our original power to command creation has merely been restored to us through the saving act of Jesus Christ.

After hearing these and several other similar stories from respectable people, and after being with a minister of healing who in her prayer often spoke directly to the diseased organ commanding it to be whole, I became open to the possibility that God might at some time want me to pray in this fashion.

It is no longer unusual for me in the middle of a prayer of healing to feel a gentle urging from within to speak to a diseased or hurt part of a person and ask it to receive God's love, to become whole, to begin functioning as God created it to, and to bring happiness and not pain to the person in need. And I have seen that prayer honored many times. Sometimes parts of our bodies become diseased or ill because we have ceased loving them. When this has happened a prayer of loving faith can love that bodily member with Jesus' love back into wholeness until its "owner" is able to love it himself or herself.

Claiming Jesus' Request

The third element of the prayer of loving faith is what is sometimes called "claiming the request." I would like to call it "claiming Jesus' request," for if what we request is not Jesus' plan for this person but our own, we should not be asking for it. The simple object of this prayer is to effect *Jesus'* loving will in the world. And Jesus teaches us how we can be sure that our request will be his when he says, *"If you remain in me and my words remain in you, you may ask what you will and you shall get it"* (Jn 15:7; italics mine). As we make choice after choice to be one with Christ and to form our lives by his teaching, he will become more alive in us. His thoughts will become my thoughts and his prayers my prayers. Personal unity with Christ refashions our wills into his. This is the heart of the prayer of loving faith, for this is the part that puts faith and love into action. Jesus makes the point this way: "If anyone says to this mountain, 'Get up and throw yourself into the sea,' *with no hesitation in his heart, but believing that what he says will happen,* it will be done for him" (Mk 11:23; italics mine).

First, Jesus says, command "with no hesitation." This is the follow-through of trust. If I really trust that God is on my side in this situation, then I will not hesitate or doubt the fact that he loves enough to heal. Oftentimes part of me trusts and part of me doubts. The doubting part is my "insurance." If a healing does not happen, then I can always retreat to my "doubting self" and the let-down will not be too difficult, the disappointment will not be too deep. Such fickleness does not advance us very far into God's world of love, however. Furthermore, the lack of hesitation must be "in the heart," the Hebrew way of saying it "from the very depths of my real self." My love and faith need to be simple.

Another subtle way we have of escaping the discipline of faith and love is by believing "with my mind"—i.e., knowing that God can and will heal, but letting my heart run free with fear of failure and anxiety. Jesus says I must learn to bring my heart along with my mind under the direction of his love and the gift of faith in him: ". . . but believing that what he says will happen. . . ." Notice, Jesus does not say "can happen" or "ought to happen" but "will happen." It is conceivable for a person to imagine a total range of possibilities concerning the outcome of a situation, but only one of them will be the actual outcome in reality. To believe in one outcome—to believe in the Lord who wants only the best results—is an act of great potency, for it is the simple union of body, mind, emotions, and spirit focusing on one good object in the loving will of God. When a person is at one within himself, God can most easily use that person as a channel for his simple but powerful love.

To find out how the human being can most easily and successfully pray "with no hesitation in his heart" has been the search of many people. I have found very helpful a method to which many Fathers of the Church testify and which was brought to my attention by Mrs. Agnes Sanford in her trailblazing book, *The Healing Light*, viz., using the pictorial imagination.

Our society, it seems to me, is so verbal that it tends to exclude the development of the imagination in us. The imagination is seen as unimportant in a technological world. Too few children receive serious encouragement to develop their pictorial imaginations as a non-inferior means of communication. To be able to verbalize is touted as the pinnacle of expression.

Too bad for any of us who have agreed, consciously or unconsciously, with this point of view in education, for it in reality is a view of human nature and a narrow one at that. It limits and diminishes the artistic side of a person as well as the power of the art he or she creates. It is a point of view that immaturely identifies imagination with the imaginary and fantasy, and therefore with illusion and unreality. It totally excludes the possibility of the "world of the imaginal": that world of inner phantasms, thoughts, intuitions, and images that comprise the inner reality of each human being. Communication with this inner world is important to a person's happiness, wholeness, creativity, relationality, and sanctity. What can we do, then, if our imaginations are undeveloped? How can we develop them now? One way is to read highly imaginative books like *The Chronicles of Narnia* and *The Space Trilogy* by C. S. Lewis or the novels of Charles Williams. Another way is to practice visualizing or to mull over the stories of Jesus, or to record your dreams. These and many other suggestions are fully treated in an excellent book by Morton Kelsey, *The Other Side of Silence* (Paulist Press, 1976).

In the mind of the Fathers of the Church, a person's imagination is seen as the "window to the world of spirit." Just as our bodies have various senses that put us in touch with the physical world, our imaginations are like an "inner sense" that puts us in contact with the spiritual world. As human beings, of course, we are part spirit and we participate in the spiritual world. Not only do we participate in it, but St. Paul says that our real selves are hidden with Christ in the spiritual world (Col 3:3). Therefore, it is a world of far greater power and authority than the physical world, and the imagination, when it is functioning in faith and grace, informs us of the happenings of the spirit-world. That information is the complete reality about ourselves and our universe. If something is so in the world of spirit, the physical world must conform to it, though it may take some time—which itself is only a physical reality and a creature of God—to do so.

From this point of view which includes the imagination, then, we can see how a well-developed imagination could be an extremely powerful element in healing prayer. To unite ourselves with whatever way Jesus is choosing to love in this situation—the sick person made well, the broken bone becoming whole, the confused relationships being straightened out, the troubled person coming to peace, whatever Jesus sees as best—could be the simplest yet most powerful way to pray without hesitation. Indeed, does not this method easily fulfill Jesus' directive, that a man pray "believing that what he says will happen"?

Using our imagination is, furthermore, a commonsense, logical and completely human way to go about any task. If you or I want to go on a vacation, do we not first imagine it by planning it, making decisions and arrangements for it, and trying to anticipate problems? When we want to build something, is not our natural tendency, indeed our need, to imagine how it will look and how it will be put together, and even sometimes (if we are experienced builders) to *draw a picture or image* of it? Imagination touches upon an inner reality that frees our ability to make something real happen in the physical world.

It is good to reiterate at this point what was said earlier in this chapter under the second point, "take dominion over creation," and that is that what we are believing in this prayer is not what we want but what Jesus wants for this person. All of our imagining is so much foolishness if we have not first asked that Jesus fill our imaginations with images of what *he* sees will be the best solution to the problem we are praying about. For only when what we ask for is already the will of God do we have the assurance that "what we say *will* happen."

We can see, then, that to pray effectively includes imagining what Jesus sees we need or desire and then thanking God that this is what he will in fact make happen. This last point—thanking God—is also an important one, for it is *God* who heals, it is God who will do this work. For all our talking about and relying on the imaginative powers in man, it is not the imagination that accomplishes the healing, but our loving God. The imagination is but a tool God uses to put us in touch with his abundant life, his healing love. This is the point at which all natural methods of obtaining health and all systems of using only the power of the mind to improve self fall short.

For while the body and mind do have natural abilities to heal—the presence of antibodies in the blood, the ability of sores to heal and bones to mend, and the ability of the mind to relax and think its way to reality after a mental breakdown attest to that truth—and while mankind may not have discovered and utilized all of these powers for healing within our natural selves, what Jesus is ultimately talking about is infinitely above and other than the natural healing ability of the human person. Jesus' message is about touching his divine love, the source of wholeness and freedom for a broken nature. It is about letting a Person into our lives who will change a lot of what he finds, who will not only mend bodies or relieve confused minds, but who will "take out our stony hearts and put in hearts of flesh" in the words of the prophet Ezekiel—a reference, it seems to me, to a healing of the spirit of man, a mending of the very essence of that which is broken, the soul of the world, the heart of the universe broken by a diabolical betrayal of the One who had made it simple and good and holy.

Therefore, a person standing in prayer "claims Jesus' loving request" by two positive actions of the inner being, imag-

ining what Jesus would do in the situation and thanking him
for it—two actions that dispel doubt and hesitation and that
open this natural world to be touched powerfully and signifi-
cantly by the love of God, the Divine Source of all the good
we seek.

I remember a time when I learned this truth by a difficult
experience. A young woman in our community was helping
her husband at the delicatessen he operated, and in working
quickly at the meat slicer she happened to slice the edge off her
little finger, completely severing it from the middle of the tip
to the outer edge at the first knuckle. Later that night she came
to the prayer meeting, drugged even as she was with codeine
because of the pain, for healing prayer. A small group of us
gathered around her to pray in a private room where she could
lie down; and I can remember as I walked into the room the
doubts I had. Since I had not yet begun my healing ministry I
did not have much successful experience to back up my faith. I
remember thinking, "You can't expect God to grow a whole
part of a finger back, nail and all!" and "She's so drugged with
codeine she won't be able to hear the prayer anyway, so how
can it have any effect?" When I walked into the room I did not
even come close to her; I knelt in the background, allowing the
others to be in contact with her.

But as I began to pray, something that I then found to be
extraordinary began to happen. I looked at this woman lying
down, and my attention was drawn to her finger wrapped in a
large, white bandage; but my imagination fixed on another
image. While looking with my eyes at the bandage, in my
imagination I saw a little finger, quite dainty and quite whole.
Everything about it was perfect, and something inside told me
that this was an image of her finger as it used to be *and as it
would be* because that was Jesus' loving plan. It was as if I were
seeing the bandage but also through it, and not through it to
the finger as it was but to the healed finger that was God's
loving will for it to be.

The fact that the image in my mind completely outstripped my expectations of a moment earlier shocked me, and yet I could not at this moment disbelieve. My mind was fixed. I recognized this image as a gift from God to aid in the healing prayer and to bring wholeness to this injured woman, and so I thanked God. I thanked him that the image I saw was what was going to be because that was his loving will, and I thanked him for the image itself, for it was a beautiful gift that God had given to show me how to pray.

When the prayer was over (I am not proud to say), my faith left me and my doubts returned. I returned to my former attitude that God could not, or at least would not, create a new and perfect tip on that finger. A week later when I was with my community again, I did not ask about this woman's condition—I did not want to hear about how poorly her finger was mending, for I assumed all would not go well. Several weeks afterward she walked directly up to me at our prayer meeting holding her hand out in front of her. I could not avoid her and I could not avoid looking at her finger. Before I even realized what I was seeing, my stomach became squeamish because I did not want to look at a disfigured finger, especially if she expected me to tell her how good it looked. However, what I was seeing finally registered on my brain—her finger was fine. Everything about it was perfect, including the nail. There was no scar nor anything discernible that would indicate it had been maimed. She reported that it felt perfectly fine, too.

At that point I become curious about something and I asked her if I could look at her hand more closely. I had not known this woman well at this point in our relationship and I had never really observed any little details about her physical appearance, like the shape or size of her hands. As I observed her hand and finger, I realized it was the same as the one I had seen when I had prayed for her. Her hand was so dainty and slender there could be no mistaking it. God had truly brought into my mind an image of *her* hand, probably from my unconscious observations, to demonstrate to me how real his power is, and also to teach me how to pray the prayer of loving faith.

Therefore, we see that often Jesus depends quite heavily on the faith of the one who asks. Faith does not include hesitation or doubt, but is a totally positive, loving force within a person. It is a gift from God that unifies body, mind, emotions, and spirit to focus a person on the goodness and love of God rather than on the evil and sickness he experiences. What Jesus is saying to us in this passage is that the goodness of God is just as real, indeed more real than the evil before us, and when we put our faith in God's reality he has the power to make that reality victorious over the limitation that binds us.

Jesus develops this line of thought further in the next verse: "I tell you therefore: everything you ask and pray for, believe that you have it already, and it will be yours." Taken literally (and there is no indication in the text that Jesus is qualifying it in any way; rather, the opposite seems from the context to be his intention), this is a sparklingly unconventional statement. Whatever we are asking for is in our possession right now if we believe in God's love. God is a good Father, Jesus is saying, and he wants to give us all that we need. As a matter of fact, he has already given it to us. All that we need is ours to have for the believing. God is not like some enigmatic Oriental potentate whose mind is malevolently inscrutable. Rather, he is a Father who loves his children and simply gives them as their inheritance all that they will ever need. If we do not always experience having all we need, maybe the reason is that we have not confidently believed that it was there for us to use.

If someone comes over to my house on my birthday and gives me a present, beautifully wrapped and tied with a ribbon, that gift is mine. It is still mine if I leave it on the coffee table unopened for several days, although I cannot use the gift because I do not know what it is. And if I store it high on a closet shelf without knowing what it is, the gift is still mine although it is entirely useless to me.

We can treat God's gifts in much the same way, except that because God's gifts are not so definable and often not tangible we even accuse him of not giving us the gift in the first place. We would not think ourselves normal if, when someone gives us a present, we responded, "That's not really for me," or "I know that isn't a present; it's just an empty box." Yet we talk to God that way. Over and over again we think negatively when we think about God giving us something we are wanting or needing. It simply is not his way to be stingy or to hold back on one whom he loves. But we insist on thinking of God in our image—small-minded, petty, resentful, niggardly—and forget that we are made in *his* image. It would be his greatest pleasure, his greatest joy if we would believe that he has given us every gift, find out what those gifts are, and use them for our own happiness and that of others. He has told us in as many ways as he can that this is his plan, this is his idea for the world and his way for us to live.

"Believe that you have it already, and it will be yours." These are the simple words of one who knew his God as Father, one who truly believed that God cares, understands, frees, and gives, not because we deserve these things, but because he wants to do things his way, and his way is love— pure, holy, other-centered love. Maybe the reason we find it difficult to believe that God gives so lavishly and generously is that if we believe in his giving we will have to see how completely he loves us. And complete love is one thing every human being wants but also fears, for it means surrendering to that love in just as complete a way. Often we would rather hang on than surrender and thus prove what Jesus said is true: "He who finds his life (or hangs on to his life) will lose it" (Mk 8:35). God is continually leading us to experience abundant living, i.e., he who loses his life for Jesus' sake, he who surrenders to God's love and believes in God more than in "the world" with all his heart, will find the real way to live and will find the joy and meaning intended for man in this life.

Forgiveness

Finally Jesus gives his last instruction in praying the prayer of loving faith. He says, "And when you stand in prayer, forgive whatever you have against anybody, so that your Father in heaven may forgive your failings too." At first, this comment seems to be entirely unrelated to the teaching that precedes it. Indeed, at one point I investigated the possibility that it was a verse that was "lost" and randomly became attached to this part of Scripture. However, from Jesus' point of view—i.e., considering the rest of his teaching on how to live in the kingdom of God—this instruction becomes the essential pre-condition for successful prayer. A heart that lacks forgiveness is a heart that lacks God's love and cannot be used by God as a channel of his power.

In other moments of teaching, Jesus identifies forgiveness as the first step in the Christian life.

Be compassionate as your Father is compassionate. Do not judge, and you will not be judged yourselves; do not condemn, and you will not be condemned yourselves; grant pardon, and you will be pardoned. Give, and there will be gifts for you: a full measure, pressed down, shaken together, and running over, will be poured into your lap, because the amount you measure out is the amount you will be given back (Lk 6:36-38).

So many times Jesus spoke the words and did the deeds of forgiveness. How could human beings ever go through life and pretend that forgiveness is not important to God? Jesus not only clearly stated his position and told us how the Father saw our arguments and resentments, but he also forgave all those who came to him asking for forgiveness. And his forgiveness did not even stop there, but from his cross he forgave all those who were violently and cruelly punishing him even though they never asked for his love or help. For Jesus, learning to forgive is essential if one is to follow his way and live mysteriously in his very own life. He reminds us that although we do not deserve it our Father has let go of all our offenses; he does not hold them against us. He asks us, then, to do the same for each other.

Applied to this teaching about healing prayer, Jesus' attitude toward forgiveness takes on additional importance. None of us is perfect in the eyes of God, and because of our sin none of us *deserves* to have his prayers heard, let alone answered. However, we *are* heard, we *are* answered because God has forgiven our sin. When we do not have forgiveness in our hearts toward our neighbor, on the other hand, several things happen. First, as Jesus indicates in the passage from Luke quoted above, if we do not pardon we are not pardoned. Our own sin will stand in the way of our prayer being heard. Second, when we do not forgive, we make it difficult if not impossible for ourselves to believe that God will forgive the person we are praying for or that he will heal him. Thus, lack of forgiveness puts a doubt in our minds about the goodness of our God. For we are only open to understanding God's forgiveness to the degree to which we are open to forgive.

Resentments, latent hostilities, and all forms that a lack of forgiveness takes, therefore, form the greatest block to successful prayer that man can create. That is the reason that Jesus speaks about forgiving our neighbor in the context of how to pray a healing prayer.

And the forgiveness we give needs to be total and complete just like God's forgiveness of us. Jesus did not say just to forgive the little things, or just to forgive the big things. He did not exclude any people from this instruction, like "You do not have to forgive your mother-in-law" or "You can keep your favorite resentment and I will not pay any attention to it." Neither did he qualify his statement by saying "You do not have to forgive if you were in the right." He simply says, "Forgive."

Wherever I have preached, I have explained this total kind of forgiveness and have never mitigated the extent or the depth of the forgiveness he expects from us. I have done this because I know the healing and freeing power of the act of forgiveness itself. Forgiving frees the one doing it to be truly the happy and creative person God has made him or her to be.

In my first parish one of the teachers in the intermediate grades of our parish school asked the children in her homeroom which priest they would like to come to celebrate a special Eucharist with them. Since I had worked many times with this particular group it was natural that most of them asked that I come for this occasion. But when the teacher asked the ones who had not wanted me to come if they had a reason for their feelings, she was surprised to hear one of them say, "I don't want him to come because he wants me to forgive everyone, even the person who stole my bicycle." That little child was resisting the word of God, of course, and not me, and so we prayed for him that he would continue to fight that battle within himself until God won. For until that time he will not be free to trust, to relate, or to know how much God loves him.

This I know as a fact, for these are the very freedoms that have come into my life as I became willing to forgive. Like everyone else, I had stored a lot in my heart that had made me hard and crusty, untrusting, locked into myself. First, I had to replay my life in my memory and forgive all the significant people in my life who ever hurt me or who did not meet my expectations. After that, many faces and names came to mind of less important people who had hurt me. Following that experience, I was surprised to find that the person who was most difficult to forgive was myself, not only for my sins and faults, but also for things for which I had judged myself as unacceptable or inadequate—my height, my weight, my looks, my emotional and mental limitations. It mattered not how others saw me. All that mattered is how I saw myself and how I had judged myself. Forgiveness in all these situations had freed me to become whole, to know, to understand, to see, to hear, to feel, and to relate. Forgiveness, however, continues to be a day-to-day need, for no one hurts us more and therefore needs our forgiveness more than the ones with whom we daily work, play, and pray.

Forgiveness, then, is Jesus' fourth and final point in his teaching on how to pray a successful prayer. With these four points—trust God, take dominion over creation, claim Jesus' request, and forgive—Jesus lays the groundwork for learning the simple steps of the actual prayer of loving faith. With these four attitudes, Jesus leads us to a more perfect understanding of the Father and his love for us his children, and this love is the fountain out of which comes the power that makes prayer a Christian's most effective tool in his attempt to bring himself and all people to wholeness.

Chapter IV
How To Pray the Prayer of Loving Faith

Traditionally, Christians have delineated four kinds of prayer: adoration, praise, petition, and thanksgiving. The prayer of loving faith does not easily fit into one of these categories. It is more rightfully called a prayer of ministry, a prayer by which God's power and love come into a person to take care of a problem. It is a practical kind of prayer, expecting practical results.

On the other hand, however, it is related to these traditional categories. The heart of the prayer is a prayer of petition, and adoration, praise, and thanksgiving are parts of the rest of the prayer. It is surely not an "untraditional" prayer form, for as we saw in the last chapter it was a prayer that Jesus taught to his disciples. The prayer of loving faith, then, is a biblical form of prayer which is the right of every Christian to know and use so that God's loving plan for the world might be put into fuller effect.

The prayer of loving faith is a response to a problem. I believe that it is easier to pray the prayer for another, although I have learned how to pray for myself this way, mostly from necessity. Let us say that a friend has been admitted to a hospital by his doctor because of irregularities in an electrocardiogram test. The exact nature of the physical component of the problem has yet to be determined, and no one has any knowledge whether or not he has undergone any emotional or spiritual trauma. As a Christian I will want to bring the Lord to him when I visit along with my personal love and concern, so I will probably want to pray the prayer of loving faith with him.

The prayer of loving faith consists of several steps:

1. Preparation (and attitudes by which I live)
   a. Pray for guidance
   b. Pray for love
   c. Renew my commitment to forgiveness
2. Thank God for the person for whom we are praying and for his or her problem
3. See the healing love of God enter the person for whom we are praying
4. Thank God for hearing our prayer and pray for a lasting peace in and around the person for whom we have prayed

While this outline might seem a bit foreboding to the beginner, it is in practice not all that difficult to do. Truly, the flow of the prayer is quite a natural one—relaxing everyone involved in the prayer, requesting healing, and thanking God for hearing our request. However, the more we let our hearts be taught about all these steps, the more we uncomplicate ourselves to let the simple, unconditional love of God pour through us to the person who needs healing, the more effective our prayer will be.

This chapter, as much of this book, is not aimed at teaching our minds but rather our hearts. Many people with great worldly knowledge have come and gone and left their mark, and the truth they have uncovered will live forever. But "the wisdom of this world is foolishness to God" (1 Cor 3:19), for while there is truth in many places, there is salvation in only one, in Jesus Christ. The words of this chapter are meant to convey attitudes that will help us to live and to minister to others as Jesus would. That is a matter of attitude, of real feeling, of changing one's life to be like his, of dying to self and living in him; it is *not* a matter of merely intellectual knowledge, ideas to clutter and fill my brain with no effect in my life, of mere curiosity in how this or that is done.

The goal of this chapter is to help us to love as Jesus loves, for his love has power to make lives whole as well as compassion for the brokenness of our lives. As we pursue these different attitudes, then, it would be well for us to remember that what we are talking about is a particular way of living the Christian life, a way that ministers to others' needs. To do that we must necessarily hold up ideals to reach for, ideals of perfection in love. God, however, does not demand that we reach such perfection before we can begin to minister to and pray for others in this way. Such a requirement would be foolish on his part, for if it were in effect, he would have no ministers to speak and act in his name. What he asks is that we learn and try, praying to him to bless and multiply our efforts and to honor our prayers. He, after all, is the healer; we are only the ministers or channels of this healing love in the world.

Guidance

Remembering our example, then, of visiting our friend with a heart ailment, the first thing that I will want to do is to pray for guidance—guidance as to what exactly will be the object of my prayer, what I am going to pray for. It cannot be emphasized enough that this is the most important part, for without directions from God my prayer is going to be fruitless. Our first inclination often is to rush in to "do everything we can." But to rush is not God's way. When we are praying the prayer of loving faith we must always remember that we are God's ambassadors, and so our direction and guidance must come from him. If we ask what to pray for, God will tell us, often quite specifically and directly, and when we are sure that what we are requesting is already God's will for this person at this time and place, then our prayer will be effective. In prayer ministry we must never assume God's will. That would be pride as well as foolishness, for anyone who knows God knows that he indeed does write straight with crooked lines. As he has told us through his prophets, our ways are not his ways, and when we are praying for another we are trying to effect *his* way, *his* loving will for this person. And there is no better way to find out what someone wants than to ask him.

We know and believe that God's general will is for the abundant life of all people; he did not make us to be unhappy but rather to praise him by being fully alive, as St. Irenaeus said many centuries ago. This abundant life that God wills for man usually includes much healing—but not in *all* situations, not only at the time *we* want to pray for healing, not necessarily through *our* prayer, and maybe not *first* of the malady that seems most obvious to *us*, e.g., a physical ailment. In other words, although God's general will is constant and known, his specific will for this person, this time, this situation, and this problem is unknown—unknown, that is, until we ask him and he tells us. That is the reason we must always first pray for God's guidance, asking to see the situation from his point of view, enough, at least, so that we will know how it is best to pray at this time. In this way our prayers will be effective and will not disappoint.

How does God's guidance actually come to us? The process is really quite natural. Let us return to our example of the friend in the hospital with a heart problem. Often, even before I go to visit my friend, just in thinking about our coming visit, I will say to myself, "When I get there, how am I going to pray?" Especially if the exact nature of the illness is uncertain, as in our example, this thought might easily become a prayer: "Lord, show me what you want done in this situation; show me how I should pray." Quite frequently some thoughts or inspirations will come before I even enter the room.

But these thoughts could easily become pre-conceived

notions that limit my prayer and limit God's power if I should regard them as God's absolute and final word. They should never take precedence over the facts I find out from my friend in the actual visit. I can walk into that room praying that the Holy Spirit will reveal to me through our conversation what needs God's attention most at this time. If I visit with my friend lovingly, willing to listen to him and give him my time, and gently search all the possible sources of the problem, God will honor my prayer and bring to my attention what needs healing. Sometimes, if the person to whom I am ministering is actively engaged with me in finding the area that needs healing, I will invite him to pray with me for a while, that God's light will shine on our conversation. Then during the conversation I listen "with one ear to the Holy Spirit and with the other to the person," as a friend of mine once said. I listen to what this person says, to how he says it, to what he does not say. I am lovingly, non-judgmentally present to him, and as a fellow Christian I also take that next, all-important step of entering into his pain with him. Then, feeling compassion for him in a Christ-centered way, I have opened myself to hearing God who is all-compassion within me leading me in my quest to help my friend.

For example, as I pray with my friend who has a heart problem, God's guidance may lead me to understand that his problem may not be merely physical but may have an emotional or spiritual base. Maybe there is tension which his body has focused on his heart due to a great sadness or a deep resentment carried for many years. Maybe he feels insecure in his job or his marriage. Thus, in praying for him as well as in talking with him, I would do well to surface the issues that I believe God has revealed to me, first to see whether or not they correspond to the facts of his life and then to use them as a direction for my prayer.

On the other hand, God may guide me in an entirely different way, telling me of some preliminary issue that has to be dealt with before the real and deeper conflict can be faced. On this visit, God's plan for my ministry might seem quite small, yet in faith I believe that it will be used by God in the hours and days my friend has to think things over to bring him to a new freedom for accepting God's healing love. On my next visit I will again need to ask for guidance so that I know how to proceed according to God's plan, maybe to pray for healing of his inner self, maybe to pray directly for a physical healing, whatever God may see as best for him.

Many of a person's problems are often unknown even to him, let alone to me as I first meet him or first talk to him about his problems. The Holy Spirit can and often will expeditiously reveal to both of us the root cause of a problem and how it may be healed as I am willing to do what Christ would do in this situation—to listen, to love, to hold back all judgment, to feel with, to believe in a greater power than pain and evil, to pray. Also, after talking and as I begin the prayer of loving faith, I pray one last time for guidance, something along this line, "Lord, grant me and my friend all the gifts we need to pray the perfect prayer you want prayed for him today." With this prayer I have again placed the emphasis on God's will and away from my will, my vanity, or my need to pray "successfully."

I remember a situation where this emphasis on seeking the guidance of the Holy Spirit was especially helpful. I had arisen one morning, my head a little foggier than usual, and found my way to church to celebrate Mass. After Mass I was heading straight for the dining room where that first cup of coffee would be waiting when the secretary intercepted me and said my appointment was in my office. "My appointment!" I thought. "What appointment?" In the confusion of the morning I had forgotten to consult my calendar which would have prepared me for the lady who had come to see me. Since she already had been waiting for a while, I went in to see her even before smelling the coffee.

This was a woman I had counseled for several sessions already, so I felt comfortable in my plan to ask her if she wanted a cup of coffee in the office with me. No sooner had I walked in and sat down, however, than she blurted out nervously, "Father, I've come here today with the most important problem of my life." No coffee today. "What is that?" I said as gently as I could. "Father, I live with this most horrible fear of death eight months out of every year. It has had a powerful grip on me for about two months now, and I can't stand it any longer."

There we were—she with an overwhelming need and I with feelings of total inadequacy. I could barely get my tongue to move in the right direction, let alone counsel someone on her overwhelming fear of death. Out of my necessity and in my naiveté I then uttered one of the wisest things I have ever said in my life. After asking her if she had any idea where this fear came from and receiving a negative response, I said, "Let's pray for some light on the situation."

We prayed, and it was not very long—maybe thirty seconds, maybe a minute—when the words came into my mind, "Her grandmother died when she was six." This, I must admit, was the most explicit guidance I had ever experienced, and, frankly, it surprised me. Not wanting to put thoughts into her head, however, I broached the topic cautiously. "Tell me," I said, "did anyone important for you die when you were young?" For a moment she just sat there, and finally with a start she replied, "Why, I had almost forgotten, I suppose because I wanted to, but yes, my grandmother died when I was six."

Then she told me the whole story. She had loved her grandmother very much. Since both of her parents were alcoholics, her grandmother was the only person who touched the reality inside the little girl. When her grandmother became seriously ill her parents would not allow the little girl to visit her out of fear of disturbing the grandmother, and the little girl became confused and sad. But when the grandmother was at the point of death in her bed at home, all the family gathered around in the old-fashioned tradition and the little girl saw her grandmother again, but this time she was gasping for breath and emaciated. Seeing her beloved grandmother in such great pain was so horrifying for the little girl that she ran out of the room crying. Her father, for reasons of his own, ran after her and dragged her back to her grandmother's bedside, and he forced his little daughter to watch this loving figure of her earliest childhood memories take her last breath.

When the lady finished telling me the story she was deeply distressed, sobbing and even moaning with the pain from the past which she had blocked out for over forty years. The inspiration of guidance had opened her up to a profoundly important memory from which she needed to be freed, but something definite and powerful needed to be done quickly to bring her from her inner pain into real freedom and wholeness. So I knelt by her side to pray.

Again relying on the Lord to follow through his initial guidance with a prayer that would heal, I took all the details of the story as she had related it to me and used them as the basis of the prayer; but as I retold the story I included the presence of Jesus in the scene. Believing that through the life, death, and resurrection of Jesus this woman had already received every blessing that she needed in this situation, my prayer imaginatively verbalized those blessings in the form of Jesus' presence with her, comforting, protecting, explaining, loving the little girl within into wholeness and away from fear.

As I prayed I saw in my imagination under the guidance of the Spirit and therefore spoke aloud how Jesus was with the little girl the first time her mother denied her access to her grandmother's room. Jesus was standing at her side with his hand gently on her shoulder as they both listened to her mother tell her that her grandmother was too sick to be visited. Then the little girl turned to Jesus as he explained in language just right for her what was happening and why, and the confused look left her face and she was at peace.

In the days and weeks that followed I saw that Jesus took her grandmother's place, playing with her and talking with her about the things that she needed to hear and the things that pleased her. So again using the Spirit's guidance, I verbalized this picture in great detail, speaking what was given to me in my imagination by the Spirit. I spoke of Jesus playing with her toys with her on the floor of her bedroom; I spoke of Jesus holding her in his lap to love her and let her love him; I spoke of Jesus letting the little girl cry on his shoulder for her grandmother, and of Jesus holding her close so that she would not be afraid, drying her tears, and bringing a gentle smile to her lips through his love for her.

Then I saw Jesus walk with her into her grandmother's bedroom at the time of her death. When she ran out and her father ran after her I realized under the guidance of the Spirit that Jesus ran out too to protect the child. Jesus took the child by the hand and led her into the room, but then he let her bury her face in his clothing and cry desperately as he stroked her hair and enfolded her in his strong arms; and she turned to look at her grandmother only when she was ready to. With Jesus' strength and tenderness to support her, she could finally look at her dead grandmother and feel peace.

It was while I was praying this last part of the prayer that the lady cried most violently, but I had a sense that she was accepting the love that Jesus had offered her long ago in this situation. At the time she was too confused and unprotected due to her parents' illness to receive the love into her heart, but on the day of this prayer she opened herself to that long-waiting love, and it made her whole. She herself had pushed the experience from her consciousness because it was too painful to handle alone as a six-year-old girl; and after the prayer was finished and she was at peace, the lady assured me that in her own estimation not a thousand hours of counseling would have brought forth that experience into consciousness. But under the guidance of Jesus she was ready to face that experience, so he saw to it, therefore, that it came forth and that someone else knew what to ask. When God's loving will says something shall be so, it shall be so. And he will give all we need for us to do our part in accomplishing it, if we yield to him, submit to his guidance, and use that guidance in gentle love.

Love

The second step in the prayer of loving faith is to pray for love, for love is the true healing power in the world. It is God's love unleashed on the world that has saved us from our own destructiveness and holds the power to heal us of illness. In praying for love we pray for two things—that the person being prayed for feels my love for him, and that through my love Christ's perfect healing love will come to him. It is important, then, that as we begin to minister to people through prayer we make a decision to love all people who need our help. This decision has many implications for the way I will think, feel, and act with a person whom God sends to me for prayer. Among them is respecting the individuality of each person and being gentle with all people. All that God asks of any of us is that we love one another. He says that if we do that much he will do the rest—the transforming and the healing, giving us abundant life.

Praying for love, for the gift of love, then, is something that begins long before I see the person for whom I will pray. It is an attitude I choose to nurture and develop within my life. And the same is true of the decision to bring the love of Christ with me into my ministry, for, truly, it is not *my* ministry, but the Lord's. If I did not actively choose to love others *so that* the love of Christ could flow through me to them, I would be running the risk of falling into the subtle, prideful temptation to love others so that they can see how well I love or so that they will love me in return. These might always be thoughts present in my mind, but when they become motives for praying they rob me of my union with Christ and they rob my prayer of its power to effect Christ's wholeness.

A friend of mine once taught me that if we are having problems loving a particular person or people in general, we should pray for the gift of love from God for that person or for all people. To our surprise and chagrin God will give it to us. Then, however, we will have the responsibility to use our gift generously. After all, what would please God more than to give the gift of love?

Agnes Sanford, who in my estimation is the first lady of healing, teaches that the Holy Spirit is sheer, unadulterated power, a flow of compassionate energy from God to men. By choosing to love with all that is in us, and by submitting our pettiness and selfishness to the gift of love from God, we become channels of that Holy Spirit energy which creates and recreates the world. The re-creation of the world is what we sometimes call healing. Love is God's motive for making us and for repairing the damage that happens to us throughout life, and so love must be our motive for being God's ambassadors. One of the most corrosive alternate motives that has come into me at times in my ministry is to pray in order to show the power of God to others. It is a most laudable thing that God's name be praised and his healing power be appreciated by all his people, but this motive is not what is needed for healing prayer. Maybe that is true because so often pride attaches itself to such a motive: they will all see God's power— but a little rider tags along—and they will see who brought it to them. No, our motive of love must be centered on the person for whom we are praying and on his welfare, for that is God's motive. To pray from any lesser motive will block the healing power of God. Indeed, I should be happy if the person for whom I pray is healed but forgets my name; my happiness comes from doing God's will. And so it is well at this time to renew our decision to love this person and to pray with only one purpose in mind—that he know God's love more deeply.

Forgiveness

For many of us, or on certain occasions as the Spirit leads, it might be well at this point also to renew our commitment to forgiveness, giving and receiving it. A forgiving heart is a pre-condition to praying a successful healing prayer, especially if during part of that prayer we are going to lead the person with whom we are praying to forgive and be freed as well. All of us find challenges in life that test our willingness to forgive. And most of us come to a certain point in life realizing that we have a backlog of resentments built up from over the years. These resentments in the minister of healing, past or present, should not be dealt with for the first time while praying with another, but need to be resolved in counseling and prayer that he seeks out for himself. And this may not always be an easy or quick task. In my own case, I took approximately three years to clear up the greater part of my backlog of unforgiven hurts. During the final year and a half of that period I was praying for healing in others, so it would seem to me that what God is looking for in our hearts is the sincere desire to forgive, the decision to forgive. We may find it helpful, then, especially during the time we are resolving long-past resentments, to renew our commitment to forgiveness every time we pray for another.

And while we are clearing out our logbook of resentments, we often find that a habit of unforgiveness persists in us into the present. It is the pain from the rejection of a week ago, the misunderstanding of yesterday, the angry words of today that are most present in our minds and hearts, and are sometimes quite difficult to forgive sincerely. To remember these situations and the people who were involved in them and to make the decision to want to forgive them before praying the prayer of loving faith frees me spiritually (although not necessarily emotionally, for that freedom usually accompanies the act of forgiving itself) to pray with confidence. I would venture to say that, forgiveness being such a difficult attitude for many people to maintain consistently, an unforgiving heart and a lack of renewing the decision to forgive before praying are two of the most common reasons that people find it difficult to learn how to pray successfully.

Up to this point we have been reviewing steps that are important but preliminary to the actual request for healing. From this point on, however, we enter the heart of the prayer of loving faith, which in essence is quite simple. After praying for guidance, love, and forgiveness we come to the second major step, thanking God for the person with whom we are praying and thanking God for his or her problem.

Thanksgiving

In Scripture St. Paul encourages us to pray in thanksgiving for all things. This may seem to be strange counsel when we consider the great variety of evil that can befall even one human life, yet there is wisdom in Paul's advice. For when we pray in thanksgiving we unite ourselves with God and therefore with his liberating power.

The notion of praying in thanksgiving for each person is easier to understand, so we shall consider it first. To pray to God thanking him for the life of the person with whom we are praying, thanking him for every part of this person because God made each part of him with devotion and care, thanking him for loving this person and for giving him the dignity of being a child of God, thanking him for redeeming this person's life and being present to him, thanking him for the privilege of being able to know this person and pray with him—these words are not only the most profound truth upon which the rest of the prayer will be based, they are also a beautiful means by which this person's faith in God's love for them is built up. And it is helpful for the minister of healing to have the person with whom he is praying in a positive state of mind, for he is then better able to accept and cooperate with the prayer.

It is important, however, that the person who prays says these words sincerely, believing in his own heart the truth of what he is saying not only for this one person he is helping, but also for himself and for all people. Perfection is not what we are looking for in this area but direction—i.e., that sincere thanksgiving is the direction and goal of the life of the person who prays. If we are to be sincere in our thanksgiving prayer, we will be dealing with our own negative attitudes toward ourselves: the ways we judge ourselves, hold resentments against ourselves for sins after God himself has forgiven them, think less of ourselves because of our inadequacies. Unfortunately, the list for most of us could go on and on.

God, our Creator, our Savior, the One we call Lord— i.e., the One whose word we have pledged ourselves to spread—has made us as we are and loves us as we are. Yet we continue trying to remake ourselves before we will give ourselves acceptance. To be able to thank God for the person with whom we are praying, then, means to be able to thank God for myself and for all people; and, most simply understood, thanking God for people means accepting them as they are and saying, with God, "That is very good" (Gen 1:31).

Prayer in thanksgiving for this person's problems follows fairly easily when we truly understand what it means to thank God for persons. We know that God does not make the evil in our lives, for God is not capable of making evil. Therefore, he did not make our sickness, our problems, or our anxieties. But while God did not make these things, we can still thank him for them because he uses them to come more deeply into our lives and to bring us closer to him. God does not make us broken but he does repair our broken parts, and thus enters our lives and leaves the mark of his special touch upon us. The things that God does for us soon become the most special parts of our lives, the parts we are excited to tell other people about. In this way, God takes the poorest parts of us, our weaknesses, and redeems them, gives them a whole new value. Where by ourselves we could only find despair and embarrassment, God brings the dignity of his presence and holy kiss. Another way of saying this is that the Holy Spirit does not see problems, he only sees opportunities to love us more. We thank God, then, that this situation that we call a problem is actually an opportunity for him to love this person again.

As we return for a moment, then, to our example of our friend in the hospital with a heart problem, I know that God does not see this condition as a problem at all. Rather, he is going to come into this situation to bring my friend closer to him by showing him his love. Therefore, I do not feel hesitation to pray to God thanking him for my friend, for all the unique parts of his life, and especially for this very heart ailment which has brought him into the hospital. I pray, thanking God that he does not leave his child in despair but will come to my friend to manifest his glory and love, performing a total healing not only of the ailment but of its causes as well, leaving my friend more whole than ever. I thank Jesus that he comes into my friend's life not as an impersonal judge but as a servant, a repairman, willing to mend his heart, for it is broken. I thank him that he also has the wisdom to help my friend throw out of his life what is useless and encumbering—sin, resentments, doubt, despair, selfishness. Truly, when we take on an attitude of sincere thanksgiving all life changes meaning—what used to be despicable becomes a shining vessel of love; what used to be considered so important in our eyes is seen as it truly is. Thus does thanksgiving exercise its power to open us up for healing and wholeness.

Request for Healing

Suitably prepared, we enter the next stage of the healing prayer, seeing the healing love of God entering the part of the person that needs it; and we again thank God for sharing his love in such a powerful way. This part of the prayer of loving faith is the heart of the prayer, the request for healing, or "claiming Jesus' request," as it was called in the last chapter. Remember the Scripture passage we were using from Matthew concerning this point: "If anyone says to this mountain, 'Get up and throw yourself into the sea' *with no hesitation in his heart* but believing that what he says will happen, it will be done for him" (Mk 11:23; italics mine). Not to hesitate in my heart, in other words not to doubt—that is the difficult part. In asking for healing we are defying our own past experience of how illness is resolved; we are defying some of the commonly accepted ideas from the world of practical science and medicine; we are defying the feelings of despair, hopelessness, confusion, and fear that illness brings to us. In the face of all that, to pray "with no hesitation" is a tall order indeed.

It takes practice. Agnes Sanford in her great book *The Healing Light* repeats the importance of starting with small requests to build up confidence, and then to move on to larger and more consequential needs. To repeat the prayer in many different circumstances, to see it work—this builds confidence and eliminates hesitation as nothing else can.

But that is not all. The world has given us a mindset, a point of view about health and illness that is wrong but very powerful. To offset this erroneous attitude an equally strong potential must be brought into play. That is the reason that the heart of the prayer of loving faith centers on the gift of our imagination, that powerful inner quality by which we create and experience the creativity of others. The power of imagination can offset the power of the world's erroneous view of how illness is resolved. As a "forgotten function" for many of us, our imaginations will need to be developed more and more finely to pray this way.

It is best to claim Jesus' request as imaginatively as possible, to fix in our minds under God's guidance a picture, for example, of the person we are praying for and the healing light of God coming from his hand to that part of the person which is ill, maimed, or troubled. We ought, of course, to ask God for inspiration for our imaginations at this time so that they will be active and so that the images that most directly correspond to what Jesus is doing will enter our minds.

It is important, also, to "speak the image forth," to put it in words and to describe out loud what we see in our minds. As we speak what we see, our words become a *full* reality and we activate our own faith in what God will do (for faith is not true faith in us until we have "put ourselves on the line" for it). As we speak what we see, our words also enter the consciousness of the one for whom we pray and they build his faith; and they enter his unconscious to reside there as a long-lasting source of believing and positive thinking. (We must always remember, however, that God does not *need* images to heal; recalling the prayer of the child in its simplicity, we bow to God's authority to use whatever channel is available to him to accomplish his will.)

The image that God gives us in our imaginations is the one we speak forth, even though we may not understand it at first, for the image that God gives will be the true image, the picture of what *really* happened in God's eyes. Only it will be the best suited to the healing of this person from this problem at this time. Each person who prays healing prayer starts by learning from and often mimicking someone else (this is another way to stimulate the imagination), and then growing in the use of his or her own gift of imagination, so that after a while images become very personal expressions, from the deepest parts of his or her creative self. If we believe with the writer of Genesis that God looks at man and proclaims "This is very good" (Gen 1:31), then it is not difficult to believe that what comes from the deepest parts of man, what is most truly himself, has a beauty unmatched in all of creation. This unique beauty which only each individual can give from himself or herself is the best conduit for God's creative beauty, his love which heals. While we aim at developing an openness to the leading that God will give to our own unique creative imagery for use in healing prayer, we may find it helpful to know about some of the general images of healing that God has given to others; they can help our creative imaginations to unleash their own uniqueness to use in service to the Lord.

As mentioned above, whether we are praying for the healing of an external or internal physical problem, an emotional disturbance, or a spiritual difficulty, we can, as God leads and guides, fix an image of the person in our minds and see the healing power of God enter as light, recreating, energizing, renewing, gently caressing the part of the person that is broken. If we are praying for an emotional or spiritual difficulty, our image of the person may be a symbolic or realistic representation. To see the person as a child needing help, to see him as a flower coming to bloom, to see him as a precious gem growing bright are all possibilities. Seeing the person depressed by a problem, then as God takes the problem away seeing him filled with life, joy, and enthusiasm, is another.

When a physical illness has put a person in bed, a beautiful prayer is to imagine him without his illness, fully healthy, active, and lively, maybe even running, jumping, enjoying life to the full. If a particular part of the body has been injured, damaged, or diseased, we can be led to picture that organ, if it is internal, as well as our medical knowledge will allow, but to picture it whole and healthy; or if the diseased part is exterior such as a limb, we can imagine the person with full use of the limb again.

When praying for someone who is blind or deaf, I will often see God's love as light and energy filling the eye or ear; I picture it as detailed as my medical knowledge will allow, seeing that energy travel over all the nerves, restoring them fully all the way back into the brain to that part which controls the impaired function. Then I see God's love as light fully energizing that part of the brain, restoring all the cells to perfection. I "speak forth" all these images in careful detail. When I am asking God to heal an attitude or a habit, I will picture the healing love of God as light in the brain.

Some physiologists explain that every experience and thought is recorded in the brain by means of a mild electrical current which causes a kind of "groove" in the cortex of the brain. An attitude or habit is caused by a repeated action causing a current to run over a groove many times making it deeper and deeper. As I am praying with a person asking God to heal a destructive attitude or habit, I will often visualize God's love as a kind of electrical current more powerful than our natural one that washes over the old groove providing the potential for it to be deactivated, and also creating new and constructive attitudes and/or habits of thought, feeling, and behavior.

The Use of Imagination

Praying in this manner may seem infantile or childish to some. It is possible for it to be misinterpreted by those who want to do so as an oversimplification of the complex process of healing and change. However, it is not that at all. This kind of prayer begins to activate or release the potential for quick healing or change with which everyone is born.

But it is not an entirely human process, either. God's divine love is also entering the person for a specific purpose, and that love is the greatest assurance that good will come to this person where he needs it the most. God's love is another, more powerful source of healing and change, entering as it does all parts of a person bringing freedom and wholeness to him.

Rather than saying that using the imagination in prayer is childish, I like to say that it is childlike. It is a method that uses all the potential within a person, not just that which is accepted by our over-rationalized culture, to bring good to himself or another. Using the imagination in prayer is also an ancient and venerable method of praying, suggested by the Fathers of the Church as well as many other great saints of all centuries; anyone who begins to pray with intensity and fervor as the saints did soon understands the necessity of using every part of himself to come in contact with the Divine.

Also, a question that many have asked is whether it is proper only to speak out those images that come spontaneously into the imagination, or whether one may pray "general images of healing," images that would be appropriate to the situation of the person for whom we are praying. It seems to me that both ways are acceptable if used with wisdom, gentleness, and trust only in God's guidance. As I mentioned earlier, it is a habit of mine to pray that God's love will so fill me during the time I am praying the prayer of loving faith that I will receive all the gifts I need to pray the perfect prayer possible for this person today, and especially that God will give me an extra measure of faith, hope, and love, as well as inspire my imagination with only *his* thoughts, so that the prayer may truly affect his will.

After praying in this way sincerely I trust that what comes to my mind is an answer to my prayer—i.e., it will affect God's will for that moment. Often while talking to a person about his problem or illness a thought will enter my mind of how the prayer for him could take shape. If no other guidance is given to me I will follow this leading and use the appropriate images of healing that I have learned are helpful to my faith. However, I have also had the experience that after praying that final prayer for God's gifts I have forgotten my first thoughts, and this I take as God's guidance again that he is in a sense saying "No" to my first inclination, for he has another plan in mind.

Then I pray for light; maybe I will pray in silence as long as five minutes, or however long it takes to feel the gentle stirrings of the Spirit within me guiding my way with new images, or maybe even guiding with a more specific word concerning what needs to be done. At these times I feel that the inspiration to prayer is specific to this person, and therefore I am, on an emotional level, more confident of my prayer. However, I have found that these feelings have little to do with the outcome of the prayer.

I remember how a young father—a man in my parish who was a friend—once asked me to come with him to the hospital to baptize his newborn son who was one day old. The child was born prematurely and his lungs were not entirely formed; his doctor had just informed this man that his child's life was slipping and he might die during the night. There is no need to describe the sadness and depression of that ride to the hospital. We entered the room gowned and brought the baby out of the incubator just long enough to perform a simple baptism. I had heard from others that this simple rite often saved the life of a child, so I had great expectation and hope. But upon completing the baptism, I sensed that more needed to be done and I could not leave; I felt within me a stirring that told me to stay and pray for the life of the child.

I prayed seeing God's life and love entering him as light into each cell of his body, and I prayed the breath of the Spirit into his lungs, asking God that what he had started there would be completed so that the child could breathe naturally.

As I asked I saw in my imagination cells forming, completing the structure of his lungs. After about a half-hour, whatever was wrong with the child seemed to be right. There was no discernible difference in his condition; it was only a feeling I had inside. Because of the desperation of the situation, I had prayed with general images of health for the child; the images were not a spontaneous inspiration from God, and so I was less confident emotionally that I had done all that God was asking. Yet it no longer felt like there was a need for us to stay, and we left in a few minutes. The life force of that child began to strengthen that very night, and today when I see him screaming and playing, a sense of wonder at God's healing love fills me completely.

On the other hand, I can remember a time when God did give me a spontaneous image telling me his will but I was not faithful to it, and the results were quite regretful. While in a small group gathered for prayer, one member asked all of us to pray for her six-year-old niece who was seriously ill. As we gathered in prayer no one seemed to be saying much; everyone was trying to get in touch with God. An image came into my mind of a beautiful brunette little girl with Jesus. Jesus was seated and the little girl was standing in front of him, her hand on his arm and his hand on her waist. Then I saw her turn and run through a beautiful meadow, while the Lord followed her, walking. The "vision" was beautiful but it was other-worldly; it had obvious overtones of heaven, and that meant that the little girl would die.

Since the lady who requested prayer was already quite distraught I did not want to upset her further, and no one wants to be the harbinger of death. So I gave in to my fears and was not faithful to the vision and the obvious symbols God was using to tell me and the woman what would be. When I spoke, my prayer was thanking God that the girl was running and jumping through a beautiful meadow and playing with Jesus. The prayer was positive and the lady who requested it was visibly relieved. However, a week later when her niece died, this woman was confused, hurt, and more upset than ever. She went for help to another lady who was present at our prayer gathering and asked why this had happened. After some talk, she finally revealed that her real confusion was that God had misled her through my prayer. The lady who was ministering to her "covered" for me and reminded her that my prayer had visualized the girl with Jesus and that there was not an image or a word indicating that she would be restored to her mother. The prayer had said she would be happy with Jesus and indeed that was completely true now. This explanation helped the lady to understand a little bit, but it did not make up for the confusion and hurt she had experienced for days, not to speak of the comfort I had denied her by not preparing her for her niece's death as God had obviously wanted me to do.

I was correct in assuming that the vision spoken in its entirety would have upset this lady, but if I had wanted to I could have spoken it gently, describing in detail the beauty of the meadow and the joy of the girl's new relationship with Jesus—all of which were quite clear in my imagination. Further, I could have sought out this woman right there in the meeting or afterward to talk to her gently and comfortingly about the vision and prayer. But I let my fear of death and my fear of upsetting another control me. And, if I am to be completely honest, I did not want to become involved in this woman's problems to such an extent. My own lack of willingness to feel concern for another and to care for her, plus my fears surrounding the topic of death, combined to undo me. Later, the lady who had explained what I had said simply told me the whole story, not knowing, of course, that there was a part of the vision I had not revealed. The incident became an important lesson for me.

It is not as important whether we use a general image of healing out of a feeling of desperation or we speak forth one that comes spontaneously into our imagination as it is to *follow God's guidance*. When we are praying for another we are a tool in God's hands. To some this image is odious because it implies utilitarianism on God's part and makes us into a *thing* in God's hands. But nothing could be further from the truth. For it is a great dignity to be in relationship with God, and an even greater one that God would minister to another and love another through us. Although God "uses" us in this sense he in no way depersonalizes us, but rather he manifests himself through our very most personal characteristics to be a channel of his grace. If we are to be a tool we are to be an obedient one, however. The hammer does not rebel from the carpenter just because its job is to hit; inanimate tools without wills are easy to manage. God is glorified greatly when we who have wills are supple and obedient in his hands, too. Then we are helping to bring wholeness to the world through the power of Christ's cross.

What *is* important as we pray the prayer of loving faith and use our imaginations is that we flow with God, being honest with him and with ourselves. As we have seen, to flow with God certain knowledge sometimes is helpful; at others what is needed is greater virtue; at others we will find ourselves realizing that we cannot pray with others until we ourselves have someone pray with us for healing, and a willingness to be humble before our God is an absolute necessity.

There are many authors and speakers who can help us increase our knowledge about healing. Two people I have found unusually helpful, especially in the area of understanding the imagination, its powers and its symbols, are Morton Kelsey and John Sanford. Several of the books of these men explain the inner workings of the imagination in prayer and in dreams, and they help us to understand the depths of the powers of our unconscious and how God enters us there for our redemption.

Many times our own ministry will bring us face to face

with our own need of healing; for example, as in the last story related, my own fears of death and of disturbing another and my disobedience to God were signs to me that I needed further ministry in these areas. It is important at these times to have a counselor or a community to whom we can turn. If we have already faced this situation we can more easily understand why Jesus sent his disciples on their first preaching and healing mission two by two. To be alone in the ministry is deathly. I do not know of anyone whose faith, hope, and love can grow as it should, or even endure, without the aid of Christian friends who can be trusted with the important elements of our own spiritual life. If we try to walk alone, we will fall apart somehow—physically in illness, emotionally in breakdown or at least in a lack of personal growth and subsequent fulfillment, or spiritually in misdirection. We need the aid of others to minister in God's name. That is one reason God has always established communities and not lone individuals in his name.

Returning to the example with which we began this chapter, then, as we begin to pray for our friend with a heart ailment, we remember to use our imagination as creatively as possible, placing it under God's supervision and inspiration, praying in gentleness, love and truth. If we encounter any difficulties within ourselves, we do not try to deal with them at this point but rather note them for a future session with someone we trust. We "speak forth" the images our imagination yields in careful detail. We may see in our imagination a simple physical image of a heart filled and surrounded with the healing light of God. We may see that the real problem is with another organ of the body and pray for it. Our images may be ones of seeing our friend resuming his normal life with all of its duties, filled with the vigor of life.

The healing images may, however, relate more to emotional or spiritual struggles, helping us to lead our friend to forgiveness of someone toward whom he has had a long-standing resentment. Maybe the one he needs to forgive is himself for a mistake he has made or for a failing for which he has long accused himself. Maybe God wants to open him up to sharing his problems with others and not keeping all his tension within; in learning this new way God wants to open him to receiving as well as to giving love. Thus we may have an abstract picture in our minds describing how tense and lonely our friend has felt carrying the weight of life alone, and then we see God's love entering bringing peace and relaxation to his heart. Whatever images we pray, we do so in the belief that each image has a twofold purpose—to place in the unconscious of our friend positive images of healing through faith, and to be a channel for the divine compassion of God's healing love. "This prayer, made in faith, will save the sick man" (Jas 5:15).

As we pray our imaginative prayer of loving faith it is also helpful to practice the scriptural tradition of the laying on of hands. Having some kind of gentle physical contact, for example the praying person placing his hand on the shoulder of the person for whom he is praying, has many positive effects, not the least of which is a non-verbal communication of concern, understanding, support and peace. For this reason, then, the laying on of hands should only be done with the permission of the person for whom the prayer is being prayed, and also it should only be done with gentleness, never with heaviness or any other quality that could be interpreted as authoritative. But the most important reason for some physical contact in faith seems to be a real transmission of power, God's power and energy of life. Many people who pray for healing have witnessed to this truth, reporting a feeling of power coming through their arms or hands. Similarly, people who have received prayer for healing have testified that they felt "something go through them," like energy or heat, which often comes to rest in the very part of them that is the source of their problem. And recently with advances in the field of photography, "pictures" have been taken of this energy as light, a type of aura around the hands of the person who is praying for healing which is then transferred to the diseased organ in the body of the person for whom the prayer was prayed.

Sometimes, also, some visible sign of this power may accompany the prayer for healing. Some people experience a spontaneous shaking or vibration of their hands when they pray. These visible signs, as the "feelings" of power mentioned above, are not necessary to the power of the prayer although for some they are helpful. Those whose heads are easily turned by external signs may allow themselves to think that only people with such signs have a "real" gift of healing. Nothing, however, could be further from the truth. Father Francis MacNutt, who is known internationally for his ministry of healing, once told me that he has never had such signs or feelings.

I remember a time soon after I began my healing ministry when I was one of those whose head was easily turned by such exterior signs. Barbara Shlemon was the person who first encouraged me to open up to a healing ministry, and it was natural that when I embarked on that ministry I wanted to emulate her. I listened to how she prayed, I imitated her counseling approach, I dreamed of being as filled with faith in God as she was. Barbara is one of those people whose prayer is often accompanied by a vibrating of the hands. She has said on several occasions that she does not like this particular manifestation because it seems to single her out, but I used to find it difficult to believe her when she said this. How I wanted my hands to shake like hers! How I wanted to imitate her in that way! I felt that if I had that particular manifestation it would be a ratification of my ministry by God. In retrospect I see how immature and foolish these thoughts were, but they were real at the time.

A few months passed and my wish was granted. Who

knows whether I willed it into being or whether it was a gift from God? All I know is that I was happy. But I was also attached to this exterior sign; if it did not manifest itself on a particular occasion I had trouble believing that God was working through my prayer. How easily our heads can be turned by non-essential things!

One day a lady from my parish called me and asked for an appointment to see me; she said that she heard I could help people and she really needed help fast. This was an unusual but long-awaited occurrence, for people in my parish at that time were not overwhelmingly accepting of a healing ministry, so I was tremendously heartened by this request. The time for the appointment came and the lady revealed her problem—she had a tremendous fear of flying in an airplane and her husband wanted both of them to vacation in Hawaii. I listened and then told her what I could do for her, i.e., pray for her and ask God to heal that fear by replacing it with his love. She was open to this approach, and so I explained to her what I would do and how I would pray, so as not to frighten her further. As I began to pray, however, an inspiration within me told me that I was not to let my hands vibrate as they usually did, but to restrain them, for I was in charge of that gift as I am of all my gifts. (God never makes us do something against our wills, but always gives us a choice whether or not to use the potential he gives us.) I was so attached to this manifestation of God's power, however, that I did not want to believe what I was feeling. I ignored the inspiration and let my hands vibrate as I normally would. The prayer ended, and we made another appointment to follow up for two weeks from that date. The day of the appointment came and went, and the appointment was not kept or remade. Approximately a week later I happened to meet this lady outside in front of the parish school, and after exchanging greetings I asked her if she wanted to make another appointment. She hesitated, a bit confused, and then asked me, "Father, the last time you prayed, your hands shook. Was that God's power flowing through your hands?" "Yes," I immediately replied, still blindly proud of what I had done. Then she shocked me and responded, "I thought so. That's why I didn't come back, you see. I thought God's power was flowing through you, but seeing it and feeling it frightened me, and so I couldn't come back."

God had warned me, but I had not listened. Had I paid attention to God's inspiration, I might have been able to help that lady. Needless to say, the experience made me re-evaluate my attachment to this manifestation of God's power. I did not use it for a long time, and then only unawares and sparingly. God taught me that he is above such little games that we like to play with ourselves, that what is important is *that he works*, not how he shows it or how my ego gets built up from it. Within a few months I became balanced on this point, and God revealed to me my own sign that he is with me. It is not always there, just sometimes. But best of all, it is from him, not me, and it is mine, not someone else's that I have stolen. For the ultimate manifestation of God working through me is faith—the faith that I have in him in my heart—and love, which is his essence and nature. These can never hurt anyone, and no one can take them away.

Petition for Peace

Finally, we conclude the prayer of loving faith with a petition for peace in and around the person for whom we have prayed. We thank God once again for hearing our prayer, placing our trust in him to see it through to its completion. We might find it helpful on some occasions to ask God to protect the person for whom we have prayed from any disturbance that would upset the healing process. Jesus often told people not to tell anyone about the healing they had just received; and he did this not without cause, for healing is a personal touch from God. It is not to be bragged about or to be taken lightly; it is not to be used as a showy story to amaze other people. Since healing is God's action in our lives, we must respect what he has done and is doing if it is going to have full effect. Also, to profane God's sacred work in our lives disrupts our inner being and puts us out of touch with ourselves. Therefore, the protection we need is often from us, but sometimes it is needed in our relationships with others who, for example, might be unsympathetic or insensitive to the healing process. As we conclude our prayer, we continue to focus on God's love in our lives. Thus, as in the case of our friend who has a heart ailment, we have placed him in the loving hands of God, and we ask God to remain with him working for his good after we ourselves have left his presence. Besides giving our friend assurance, this prayer, like all prayers, actually effects what it says. "Ask, and it will be given to you" (Mt 7:7) is what Jesus told us.

The prayer of loving faith, then, comprises four major elements: in preparation—guidance, love and forgiveness; and at the heart of the prayer—praying in thanksgiving for the person and for his problem, seeing the love of God entering the person and thanking him for it, and concluding with a prayer for protection and peace, thanking God for the healing that is taking place.

Advice for the Minister of Healing

As we enter more and more deeply into a healing ministry and take on the responsibility of praying prayers for healing with people as they need this help, there are some points of which the minister of healing should take note. First, he must remember that having faith is the responsibility of the minister of healing, not of the person for whom he is praying. The very reason that someone needs him to pray with him is that he is not strong enough at this moment or in this situation to have faith for himself. Therefore, it is wrong to do or say anything that would make the person to whom we are ministering feel guilty for not having enough faith. To imply, for example, that we have done our best and if the prayer does not take effect it must be because of a lack of faith on his part would be a gross injustice to this person. Such a statement would also probably drive him deeper into the despair and confusion that the prayer of loving faith was supposed to draw him out of.

Second, when praying, the phrase "if it be your will" should be avoided altogether. It is the kind of doubt that enters a prayer which will rob it of much power, as well as put doubts into or reinforce doubts that were already in the mind of the person who needs God's help. Figuring out God's will should have been the first thing for which the minister of healing prays in the prayer for guidance. Therefore, to say "*if* it be your will" undercuts his faith. Sometimes, however, we are not sure *how* God's will is going to be affected; in these situations to pray that all be done "according to his will" might be appropriate. Anything else might be our subtle way of taking our "insurance" against the "failure" of our prayer.

Third, while it is the responsibility of the minister of healing to have faith for and pray for the person who needs God's help, these are the *only* things he is responsible for. As people who ask God to heal other people, we are not responsible for the outcome—that is God's responsibility and his alone. He is the one who is doing the healing, not we. All we can do is our best at loving, believing, and praying; the rest is up to God to effect according to his own perfect and loving plan for each individual. Sometimes, especially when we have experienced God doing a great work through our humble efforts and little prayers, we might be tempted to take responsibility for the healing that has happened. But we must remember always that if we take responsibility for successes we must also take responsibility for failures. Anyone who thinks about it will want to take neither. Healing gives praise to God, and if someone praises us for our prayer, we can humbly thank him for his gratitude and kind words, but give the major portion of the praise to God who rightly deserves it.

Finally, we must note that the prayer of loving faith is made in the power of Jesus; without the cross of Christ and the victory that he won there over sin and death and all their effects, we would be able to pray no prayer at all. That is the reason that Jesus instructs us: "Whatever you ask for *in my name*, I will do" (Jn 14:13; italics mine). "In my name"—what does that mean? Does it mean that we merely tack the name of Jesus onto the end of our prayer?

Scholars tell us that to the Hebrew "in my name" meant what "in my character" or "in my personality" would mean to us today. This insight would indicate that to pray in Jesus' name would mean that we need to learn to live in Jesus' character—to live as he lived. A minister of healing, then, if he is to pray in Jesus' name, will be developing his own spirituality in action and in personal prayer, letting God reveal in him his freedom, his wholeness, his abundant life. It is not that to pray for healing we *must* be saints, perfect as Jesus was. But when healing flows through us and we feel God touching others through our lives, we *want* to become saints, to draw close to Jesus and to imitate him.

The minister of healing learns to be open as all Christians should to those little, behind-the-scenes acts of charity for those with whom he lives, works, plays, and prays. He also learns the necessity of a personal prayer life—for faith, because his will be tested and challenged greatly; for strength, because praying for others is often exhausting; for courage, because many will not understand or accept what he does and will persecute him in one way or another; for understanding, because in our world there will only be one person who will truly understand how and why we do what we do, and that person is Jesus himself, the object of our prayer; and for love, because we cannot give that which we do not have.

As we pray more and more in Jesus' name, we will also find that he will do much to draw us closer to his way of life, the way of wholeness, freedom, and abundant life. We will find that in praying for others' healing, we will be finding our own. Jesus will become a part of us and transform us into him. We will then be praying through him, with him, and in him, giving glory to the Father not only by doing what he leads us to do, but also just by being who we are.

Part Two
Healing the Inner Person

Chapter V

The Need for Inner Healing—
The Human Situation

All people experience a lack of inner freedom. If there is one statement that all honest men and women could confirm it would be this one, for none of us has escaped entirely the experiences of limitation such as failure, frustration, and fear. Each of us may express it in a different way, or, due to his own personal weaknesses, may find one kind of inner bondage prevalent over others, but we all experience in common this one fact. Various authors have gone so far as to call this "*the* human situation," and, indeed, without experiencing the risen Christ in one's life, lack of freedom and bondage to weakness are the only experiences of day-to-day living that we could say mark the life of each human being.

To understand deeply that this statement is a truth, however, many people have to stop and take stock, for they are not consciously aware of their inner bondage. And the reason for this seems, when we look squarely at the issue, to be simple: the experiences of failure, weakness, bondage, and lack of freedom are unpleasant ones that most of us would rather forget than constantly attend to. So we do. We choose to push aside or push down into our unconscious psyche our negative experiences; as we "forget" about them we try to live as if they were not there. Like the proverbial ostrich with its head in the sand, we think that this painful world of negative experience has disappeared just because we cannot see it. We think of ourselves as "doing all right," "fairly happy," "not needing much help (a savior)," "able to get along on our own." While there is truth in these statements, their chief failure is that they only see half the truth, the pleasant half. And in looking only at one side of life we make a subtle but very real compromise. We settle for what we have in life rather than striving for the whole prize; we settle for second best. For we cannot change that which we do not admit is there.

But when we stop, become quiet, and look at ourselves—when we pull ourselves out of the maddening pace of our world (one of the reasons for keeping up the maddening pace in the first place is to prevent ourselves from seeing that which we do not want to see)—we will surely find within ourselves some surprising negative attitudes. Maybe we find parts of ourselves that frighten or disgust us, or that we simply do not like. Maybe we have a vague sense that our "real selves" are imprisoned, that there is a sensitive, kind, beautiful self enshrouded in a hostile, defensive, critical person whom we present every day to the world. Maybe we find we have automatic reactions of anger or jealousy or fear that come out of us uncontrollably and cause much hurt to ourselves and others. Maybe we have a vague feeling that life has lost its meaning, that we are not all that we could be, or that there is no hope for change and growth in our lives.

Maybe we have already seen and faced these things in ourselves as well as we can and attempted to improve but failed. Then we are left with the gnawing experiences of knowing that certain subjects and certain situations are too difficult for us to deal with, for they bring anxiety, fear, feelings of rejection, hurt, loneliness, and anger upon us. Maybe they overwhelm us with depression.

All of this is to say that when we look honestly at our lives and our lack of inner freedom we see that our bondage has produced pain. Feelings of being unfree and feelings of hurt are deep within all of us. And so, while few of us let others know that we hurt until we are forced by a crisis to seek another's aid, all people hurt within, all experience the inner pain of being a human being. Every person walks around in life, whether or not he allows others to know, whether or not he himself is aware, carrying a heavy interior burden of pain. Now pain in itself is not a bad thing necessarily; but when pain continues and continues, when it remains unresolved and unchanging, when it grows and rarely if ever diminishes even for a moment, then it becomes destructive. And given our human predilection for burying pain in our unconscious psyches and not dealing with it because it is not pleasant, it is safe to say that for most of us the experience of inner pain slowly tears at our personality, our dignity, our self-respect, our self-concept. The burden of pain that all of us carry drains our energy from creative and productive activity and makes us feel unworthy, guilty, hopeless, broken, and unforgivable.

This burden would be destructive enough if its effects went no further, but such is not the case. These negative feelings, now converted over a period of time into attitudes, begin to develop within us negative patterns of behavior, and our past begins to destroy our present. That which is so negative begins to want to destroy itself, and so we develop habits of self-destruction or habits of sin, for sin is that power which would prevent us from becoming who we are meant to be and would bring us down into the morass of fragmentation and isolation that comes from evil.

This unfreedom, this bondage, this hurt, this burden becomes more apparent to us as we confront honestly our negative attitudes and behavior patterns. These are very real, not imagined; just because they are not physical entities does not mean that they are not there. These forces within us are a power to contend with, a power that grows from day to day and year to year, a power that destroys, disintegrates, and inflicts pain. This burden we carry within us called "the human situation" is the accumulated effect of evil upon our lives.

"*How* does it happen?" we may well ask. Why is it that the past cannot be merely the past, gone and forgotten? From one point of view it seems unnatural that the past could affect the present so greatly. What is it that allows this burden of pain to continue in our lives from one day to the next, from one year to the next? What is it that allows hurts to accumulate over the years and continue to affect us in the present?

The answer to this question is to be found in the fact that the human brain can remember, and what it remembers can be both conscious and unconscious.

Remembering

Common beliefs among the general populace about certain capacities of the brain like remembering are far behind the truths that science has discovered. Over twenty-five years ago in 1951 Dr. Wilder Penfield, a neurosurgeon from McGill University in Montreal, Canada, began research and experimentation with remembering during the course of brain surgery. His conclusions and discoveries were used by Dr. Thomas A. Harris as the basis of his book *I'm OK, You're OK* and are also important for us in our present search. For Dr. Penfield said that his research indicated very strongly that the human psyche records in minute detail every experience we have waking or sleeping and that record is stored in us forever.

Dr. Penfield's research began with the medical fact that the brain and the whole nervous system function on a low quantity of electricity; in other words, a kind of electricity is the means by which sense information passes through the nerves in our bodies to our brain, and it is also the means by which our brain functions to compute and record this data as well as to manufacture higher forms of knowledge. Some of his experimentation consisted in taking an electrode probe which produced approximately the same quality of electrical current that the brain does and exposing it to the memory section of the brain of a patient during surgery to see whether it would influence the functioning of the brain. One of the significant conclusions of his research was that each touch of the electrode brought into consciousness a single memory, not a mixture of memories or a generalization based on particular memories. Furthermore, he found that when the probe was applied to a particular area of the memory section of the brain, the patient was compelled to focus on that memory whether he wanted to or not.

But, for our purposes, maybe his most significant discovery was that not only are past events recorded discretely and in detail in the psyche, but feelings associated with the memory are also recorded in the brain in such a way that they cannot be dissociated from the facts of the event. The kinds of memories that Dr. Penfield's probe evoked were not of major importance to the patient; rather than memories of major events these were more like the daily occurrences we all have—e.g., the patient would hear a song go through his mind probably just as he heard it on a particular occasion, or he would find himself part of a situation that developed and evolved just as the original one did. But the patient was aware that these were memories from his own life, for as the memory was evoked he was both actor and audience of it, and the feelings that he had at the time of the memory came back to him as clearly as if he were first experiencing them.

While the brain seems, then, to record a perfectly accurate account both photographically and phonographically of the experience, it is even more faithful than a high fidelity tape recorder, for the patient is also simultaneously aware of the same interpretation he gave to his experience as it first was happening. The evoked memory is more accurately called a reliving than a recalling, for it is a reproduction of the very things the patient saw, heard, felt, and understood. And all this data is present in the brain whether a person is conscious of it or not. It is also interesting to note that this scientific view of the function of remembering agrees with the psychology developed by St. Augustine over 1,500 years ago.

Dr. Penfield's work could be summarized as follows:

1. The brain records every experience we have waking or sleeping.

2. The feelings that we have with these experiences are also recorded in such a way that they cannot be separated from the memory of the experience itself.

3. Through the function of remembering a person can exist in two psychological states simultaneously, or, in other words, a person can be aware of his present surroundings and yet relive a past experience so clearly that he feels as if he were in the past too.

4. The experiences recorded in the psyche are always within us whether or not we are consciously aware of them; some of them are available for recall at any time from the function we call memory, but others are buried deeper within us in our "personal unconscious" and are available only through dreams and prodding from outside the psyche.

5. Recorded experiences from the past provide much of the data out of which today's experiences are formed, for these past experiences are recorded so accurately and implanted in us as a part of us so firmly that through them a person not only *remembers* how he felt but he truly *feels the same way now.*

The Past Is Present

So, then, we see that the past in a certain sense is not past at all, but rather it is an active part of the present. However, the past does not exist "in itself," but long after each event happened it continues to exist in the minds of the beings who have experienced it, and, most importantly, it shapes those beings and directs them. That which determines the progress and direction of those beings is the *content* of the past as it was experienced and remembered, whether consciously or unconsciously. Therefore, if the past influences the present it also influences the future—shaping, guiding, and sometimes limiting it. The past brings its own joy and pain into the present and the future. Another way of saying all this is that the little boy or girl, the young man or woman we once were still exists within us; he or she still lives and brings his or her joy and/or sorrow into our lives right now.

Maybe the most surprising truth about the human brain for most people when they hear of it for the first time is that our past lives in us whether or not we remember it consciously. Most people identify consciousness with their entire brain, but medical research such as Dr. Penfield's has given us other data. Consciousness is not the entirety of the brain at all. As a matter of fact only a small portion of the brain is used for conscious functions; the rest of the brain is either unused or functions at various levels of unconsciousness. Furthermore, the term "unconscious" as it is used in psychology does not mean the same thing as it does when we say a person was hit on the head and is unconscious, i.e., not functioning and not able to think clearly; rather it is meant to convey a type of thinking that is out of reach of the awareness of our conscious psyche in what would be called normal, day-to-day living.

But our unconscious is a very real part of us, and the processes of this part of our psyche, while not being the same as the processes we call "thinking" or "feeling" or "awareness" in our consciousness, have a logic all their own. Learning about these processes is very difficult for they are, after all, "unconscious," and so learning about them is similar to acquiring a new language—it takes time, patience, and a willingness to give the new thing to be learned the "benefit of the doubt." But learning to establish communication between our conscious psyche and our unconscious psyche is the beginning of true wisdom and wholeness.

When we forget our past experiences or choose not to remember them because they are too painful they do not drop from us nor do the effects of those memories float out of us. They sink into the darkness of the personal unconscious. One major problem with this situation is that the unconscious is the irrational part of us while the conscious is rational; therefore, when any memory sinks into the unconscious it is out of the control of the conscious. If a painful memory remained in a person's consciousness it would hurt him, but the pain would be a motive to seek a resolution to the hurt—forgiveness, comfort, healing, whatever may be needed. When a memory sinks into the unconscious, however, it does not lose its nature; rather, it continues to cause pain, but in an unconscious way, a way in which no resolution can come to the pain. So the pain continues to hurt us.

What difference does that make, we might ask, if the pain is unconscious and we cannot feel it? But we do feel unconscious pain; we feel it and express it, however, in irrational ways typical of the unconscious. Accumulated hurts may come out as uncontrollable "fits" of anger, jealousy, or depression. Accumulated guilt may be expressed in physical or psychological illness. Phobias—irrational fears of harmless or only ordinarily dangerous things—may be the result of fearful forgotten episodes in a person's history.

These kinds of pain are more harmful and destructive than the original pain that caused them, for they are more difficult to deal with and find remedies for. That is the reason that ignorance of the workings of the unconscious is dangerous to any human being. The destructiveness of the working of the unconscious comes from its irrationality and its power, for, contrary to popular belief and practice but attested to by the research of psychology, the unconscious is larger and far more influential than the conscious or the body. It should also be noted, however, that the constructive power of the unconscious, when it is harnessed through communication with consciousness, is even more powerful and influential.

In the darkness of the unconscious, painful memories attract and attach to one another, gathering force and momentum which become an energy to be acted upon. Ultimately that negative energy becomes a negative attitude, or a negative habit, or a state of ill-health which effects and limits present behavior. The effect of pain is destructive; especially when a person does not deal with his pain consciously it can "get him from behind" in an irrational reaction in which he cannot see any relationship to the pain that first caused it. Thus the source of the problem is much more difficult to find and the problem is more difficult to solve.

Then, when we consider not one or several but a lifetime of negative memories, we can see how our lives come to be controlled by so much sin, illness, depression, aggressiveness, hostility, jealousy, and warfare. The number of people that I myself have seen who have told me stories of their lives that ratify this view is in the hundreds. Not only that, but it seems to me that my own life is a prime example of this reality. The pain of being adopted was in my case a tremendous one, a feeling of being totally rejected by my natural parents. The ordinary hurts that come into any child's life were far more destructive for me, therefore, because they attached to this basic hurt so that the core of rejection grew and grew. All the while as I was growing up, even from an early age, I was aware of a tremendous anger within me—it was identified as a "mean streak" by adults—that came out uncontrollably with a blinding force.

As I grew older and found that such "meanness" was unacceptable behavior, I became more subtle in expressing these feelings; since I felt rejected, I developed an attitude of rejecting others. I rejected them before they could reject me and prove to me that I was truly worth only rejecting. And with every year I expressed my rejecting attitude in more and more complex ways. Anger and aloofness were the first signs. When I got along a few years in school, I developed an attitude

of intellectualism that separated me from others less intellectual than I. I became critical of people and situations that
did not meet my standards. In high school, when my sense of
wit and humor were developing, I managed to find many
quick, jabbing remarks that put people off and made them
afraid of me.

By the time I was in college I had also rejected every part
of *me* and of *life in general* that was not connected with the
intellect; and as I communicated these rejecting attitudes
about myself, others found me difficult to be with. All this
insight I now have, however, in hindsight—as I was living
these years I was only partially aware of these problems and I
was totally *unaware* of their origin in the hurts of my childhood including my adoption.

But I *was* aware of the fact that I was very unhappy. The
way I verbalized it then was that there was a gentle, warm,
kind and loving "me" living inside this bristly angry, rejecting
"me." But it was the outer "me" that contacted the world and
made people dislike me before they could find the "real me."
In my frustration I would become depressed and see no hope
for happiness in my life. I would sometimes retreat into a little
world of self-pity and jealousy of others who did not have to
fight the battles I fought. Sometimes I would manipulate
others in games too complex to describe; I would try to make
them like me, but I would not believe or trust their affection
when it came because I thought I had manufactured it through
manipulation. When people did become my friends I would
test their love over and over again until they failed a test; then
in my heart I could claim that their love was not real or honest.

Down deep I did not believe I was worthy of love because
most of the time I did not know and accept the "real me"
beneath the outer self that I dealt with all the time; after all, I
never saw any other self in operation except the angry and
rejecting self. My past was indeed present. I was rejected as
unlovable at my birth—or at least so I felt—and so I lived out
that unlovability and rejection every day of my life. And with

every year these negative patterns of behavior became more encompassing and more confusing. Because my past hurts were repressed into my unconscious I lived them every day, ached with them every day, and allowed my future to be limited by them. And since my hurts were unconscious or unknown to me, the solution to the problems they caused was similarly unknown.

I lived in a world of darkness and anxiety; I felt different from others and thus separated from them. I did not know whether I could ever be "normal," i.e., whether I could ever live like and feel like other people. My problems seemed to have no end, indeed, seemed to be an integral part of me, not something in me that could be resolved and changed. My state was so unhappy and unhopeful because of the effect of repressed memories in the unconscious upon my life.

The Human Psyche

To understand how my experience is a specific example of the general state we all experience inside ourselves, it might be helpful at this point to refer to a diagram devised by Morton Kelsey, based on the ideas of the great psychologist Carl Jung, to explain the human psyche; for one of the advantages of his view is that in using it we can see the relationship of consciousness to unconsciousness. First, we notice that man lives in two worlds, the world of physical reality and the world of spiritual reality. Most of man's psyche exists in and is tuned into the non-physical world. The culture of the Western world, however, has largely ignored this part of man, relating only to consciousness and ego. There are other realities in this world, too—the Holy Spirit and evil—as the diagram indicates, but by cutting off the non-material world Western man has only been able to pay attention to the ways these realities show themselves in the physical world. Thus their true

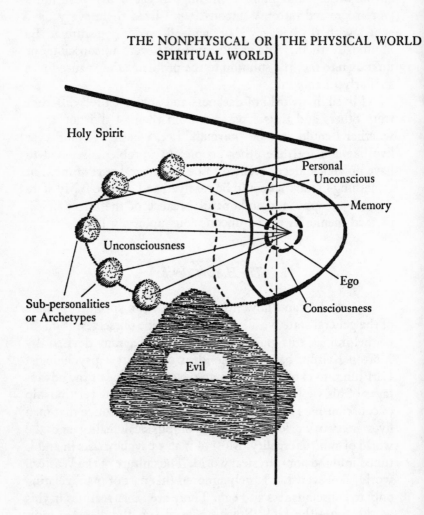

THE NONPHYSICAL OR | THE PHYSICAL WORLD
SPIRITUAL WORLD

Holy Spirit

Personal
Unconscious

Memory

Unconsciousness

Ego

Sub-personalities
or Archetypes

Consciousness

Evil

From *The Other Side of Silence* by Morton Kelsey (Paulist Press, 1976), p. 37, with additions from lectures by Kelsey.

natures—which are spiritual—remain unknown to him.

So it is this non-physical world that we must study in order to understand fully who we are. Another reason for becoming acquainted with this part of reality is that this is the part of us into which the Holy Spirit and the forces of evil come; and if we want to understand how good and evil operate in our lives we must know about the world in which they and we live together.

As we can see from the diagram, the unconscious is larger than the conscious psyche. Size here is meant to indicate power, energy, ability to influence life and also the number of forms this energy can take. A part of the unconscious is the memory, and another is the personal unconscious; these are the parts of man to which we have largely been referring in this chapter. Beyond the personal unconscious—and here we are borrowing terms directly from the psychologist Carl Jung—is the largest part of the unconscious, the collective unconscious.

Attempting to simplify this concept of Jung's without doing it injustice is a difficult endeavor. We could say that the collective unconscious in some ways roughly corresponds to what others have called human nature—those non-physical parts of ourselves, mainly spiritual or psychic *capacities* that every human being is born with. To anyone who accepts Jung's research and his writing (*The Collected Works of C. G. Jung*, 20 volumes, Princeton University Press) the existence of the collective unconscious is beyond doubt. It is a deep and, for most of us, unknown reality, the source of much of who we are. It is the home of our "sub-personalities"—what Jung calls "archetypes"; these are images which function as parts of our personalities, sometimes rising to expression and freeing the power of the unconscious in our lives into action. Among them are the shadow (the dark side of the personality), the woman, the man, the persona (the mask we wear for society), the child, the wise old person, the Self. Each of these sub-personalities or archetypes has both a positive and negative side to it. For example, the sub-personality of the child can sometimes make us playful and carefree but at other times it can be like a sniveling brat overtaking our actions; the sub-personality of the woman in a man can sometimes make him moody and irritable, at other times creative and insightful. These archetypes are the parts of us that either the Holy Spirit or the spirit of evil influences in our daily actions—the Holy Spirit, of course, bringing to the fore the positive side of the sub-personality and the spirit of evil bringing out the negative side. (For a fuller explanation of these realities the lectures, tapes, and written works of Morton Kelsey are most helpful, especially *The Other Side of Silence*, Paulist Press, 1976.)

If we are to be honest with ourselves, we must admit that the good and bad of life, the pain and pleasure of life, the creativity and destructiveness we all have experienced come in a large part from our unconscious, both personal and collective. Our memories both happy and sad, our sub-personalities with their positive and negative sides, the direct influence of both the Holy Spirit and the spirit of evil, and all of the rest of the life-force of the unconscious—these are the source and foundation of much of what we call human existence. The problem that most of us find is, as we have seen from many different points of view already, that this large and influential part of us *is unconscious*, i.e., it lives in darkness and out of touch with our consciousness, *and it was not made to live in that darkness*. We know this to be true because of what the Bible says about the creation of man and how he lived, for Genesis says that Adam lived in the presence of God, in his light.

The Effect of Sin on Our Psyche

Whatever else the story of the creation and the fall of man is trying to tell us, we know that it says that man was not intended to live the way he does today. God's plan was that man would live in intimate communion with him. In the childlike simplicity of his story-telling, the writer of Genesis says, "The man and his wife heard the sound of Yahweh walking in the garden in the cool of the day" (Gen 3:8), thus indicating that the man and woman had an intimate and comfortable relationship with God. Throughout the entire creation story God works hand in hand with and for man, talking freely with him, sharing with him, helping him. The man for his part listens and cooperates and receives graciously. For example, God gave all the seed-bearing plants and fruit trees to man for him to eat (Gen 1:29-31); God settled man in Eden to cultivate it which man did (Gen 2:15); God gives man a moral admonition for his own good (Gen 2:16-17); God was concerned that the man should not be alone but have someone he could relate with (Gen 2:18).

As we look at the kind of relationship that man had with God before the fall we see that there was no darkness in man and so he was at home with God. His life was good and simple with none of the complexities that we have been talking about as "the human situation." That was because Adam lived with God; he lived in the light of God. All of him was bathed in that light and affected by it; he listened to God and worked with God and so was happy. If all of Adam was in the light of God, that means that the part of *us* that lives in darkness, the unconscious, was not in darkness in Adam. This part of him existed, but in light rather than in darkness. In other words, it was not unconscious at all but rather available to him at all times; it functioned as a part of him as readily as any other part. It was therefore open to God's love and receptive of it, and so was strong against the attack of sickness and evil, hurt and pain, guilt and fear. This was God's plan for man—to live in dignity, freedom, and joy, to live in communion and friendship with him.

But sin changed all that. When man chose to sin he chose

to try to live by another light than God's, a light which turned out—as all lights other than God's would—to be a darkness. Sin destroyed the beautiful plan that God had designed in man. Sin made man dysfunction and turn against himself because sin drove a large part of man into unconsciousness where it became dark, mysterious, and dangerous. This dark and unconscious part of man then became a natural home for everything like itself—guilt, fear, memories of pain and unresolved hurt, energies for self-destruction. And it became a breeding ground for attitudes and patterns of behavior that relieved the tension of all this darkness by aiming it outward in the various forms of mistreatment of other people we know to be common among humankind. Indeed, the story that immediately follows the fall of man in Genesis is the story of Cain and Abel, their rivalry and jealousy, and finally the murder of Abel (Gen 4:1-16).

Personal problems whether intellectual, emotional, physical, or spiritual, relationship problems, psychosomatic illnesses, patterns of destruction of self and others all thrive in the world of the unconscious because it is dark. And the light of God's love cannot touch it unless it is *invited* in.

Another way of saying all of this is that the infant we once were, the child, adolescent, and young adult we once were, are all still living inside of us through our memory, the personal unconscious, and the powerful archetypes of the collective unconscious. As they live they still seek to resolve the problems and pains that were not adequately dealt with at the time they happened. Parts of us still seek—whether or not we are aware of these parts of us and their search—to atone for previously incurred guilt, to find solutions to unresolved problems, to experience love for all the times we needed love but it was not there whatever the reason for its absence.

Every once in a while these issues come into the forefront of our lives so clearly we can identify them and face them relatively squarely. But most of the time they remain more or less subliminal, just beneath the surface of consciousness or deeply engulfed in the unconscious, acting out their needs and desires without our full consent or approval. At these times we experience them as a heaviness, an inability to change, a sluggishness in development, a psychosomatic illness, an emotional disorder, a limitation that directly blocks growth, or a kind of behavior that aims at destroying self and others.

The best example of this unconscious dilemma that I know of—and the best example of the best solution—is a woman I have known for several years whom I call my "miracle lady," for the fact that she is alive today is truly a miracle as especially her doctor will testify. Six years ago this lady found herself at the point of death: two-thirds of her stomach and also thirty-six inches of her intestines were ulcerated beyond repair, she suffered from angina pectoris (painful constriction of her heart muscle in response to extreme tension and anxiety), many of her bones were afflicted with rheumatoid arthritis, and she had a spastic colon. The medicine the doctor would give her to treat one problem would aggravate the others, so that after treating her for a while the doctor told her husband that her case was hopeless and she had about six months to live.

While she was an energetic and creative person she found much of her life frustrating and unproductive. She had serious problems in her marriage as well as with each of her five children. Within a two-year period her mother, father, and grandfather all had died and she had suffered a nervous breakdown. Truly her life was in a total shambles by her early thirties.

It may sound like an unreal tale of trouble and woe, but one could say that in a certain sense these problems were a logical conclusion to the events of her early childhood and teen years. Her family was poor, very poor. She was an unwanted child, and her mother tried to abort her many times during her pregnancy. She lay so perfectly still in her mother's womb that her mother thought she was carrying a dead child until the very moment of her birth. Her father was a gambler, a "rambling man" whom she adored. But in reality as a little girl this child was not sure exactly who her parents were, for they all lived in an extended family situation with thirteen adults—aunts, uncles, a sister, parents, and some friends—and her sense of identity was weak and confused.

She spent her childhood feeling unwanted; for example, she remembers that when she was out and was wanted at home someone would send the dog to fetch her and lead her home by the arm. Her sister who was nine years older than she died at the age of sixteen from a rare and extremely painful disease, and most of the family's love and attention were focused on her before and after her death. The family moved frequently across the country. The end of her adolescence came cruelly, abruptly, and early when, at the age of sixteen, she was raped by one man and within a few months married by another. Her five children were born in seven years by a husband who did not communicate, who drank, and who mistreated her physically even when she was pregnant.

The physical and emotional problems that resulted in her, then, were an indirect and unconscious but nonetheless causal response to the trauma, cruelty, and pain of her life. Because she could not in any reasonable way handle so much confusion and pain, it was repressed and later expressed as illness and dysfunction. Indeed, it seems that her body and mind were destroying themselves because she had been attacked in so many different ways that she believed she was unworthy to live.

She was coming dangerously near to death. When the doctor informed her husband that she had no more than six months to live, her husband's response was to plan to sell their house and buy his wife her dream home, and they called a local real estate agent to put the house up for sale. This, however, was no ordinary real estate agent, but rather a woman who had recently come to believe in the healing power of the Lord. The sick lady, especially after the death of her dearest family members and her nervous breakdown, did not believe in God and certainly not in healing. But the woman said she would pray for her that night with her husband and her friends and she was sure that she would be better the next day.

When the next morning came the sick lady had an amazing experience—she felt no pain. At first she was not even aware of it, so long had she lived with constant pain. Then she realized and was skeptical, and finally when the comfort persisted she accepted. But she did not believe she had been healed by God. The agent continued to visit and urge her to come to a small local prayer group and publicly thank God for his gift to her, but she still would not admit that God had healed her.

Then one day her sister-in-law phoned and said that her niece was ill with a non-functioning kidney, and since both kidneys were affected seriously, she was close to death. When the real estate agent came to visit that day, she threw her out of the house, saying, "If your God is so good with stomachs, see what he can do with kidneys." The group prayed, and when the operation on the sick girl took place the doctors declared that they had made a "mistake," for they found two healthy kidneys in her body. At that point the miracle lady gave in to God and came to believe in him and his loving power to heal. Later she went to her doctor who with X-rays verified a miracle—her stomach and intestines were whole, and all signs of a spastic colon and of angina pectoris were gone.

Aside from her arthritis which disappeared in several months, her physical healing was instantaneous and complete. But many of her psychological and relational problems continued, and so she began to seek out inner healing prayer. For while the prayers of the group and the physical healing that resulted had *saved* her life, inner healing prayer for her memories and emotions would help her to *keep* her life, so that it would be of value and worth to herself and others. She struggled for months and for years through many stages of personal, inner growth. During this time tremendous gifts for the healing ministry were released in her, and to this day she has helped many people while she herself was helped by God.

As with most people, but with the miracle lady to an extreme degree, most of her psychological growth centered around the issue of her own worth and value. She did not believe she had any, and no mere words or simple one-time prayers could undo the years of trauma and confusion she endured as a child. At one point in her inner healing process she uncovered a memory from her second or third year in which her uncle had been taking her along for a walk. As they walked along the edge of a garbage dump that was a huge pit into which the town's refuse was dumped, he, in a playful but remarkably insensitive way, held her out over the pit and threatened to drop her in it. The little girl looked down into the pit and thought, "If that is where he is going to drop me, that must be what I am—garbage." The effect of the prayer that was prayed for her at that time was as powerful as any in her life, and it was the beginning of a whole new self-image.

The miracle of God's freeing love began to spread throughout her whole family as well. Not that she or any of her family live "perfect" lives—they live as other people do, but not exactly. For they have been touched deeply by Jesus and he has changed the course and direction of their entire lives.

Today I continue to see God working in the life of the miracle lady. He gives her much wisdom to understand his ways in her life and that of others. The power of faith and love shown through her have brought healing to many, many people, including myself. He has healed the psychological hurt of her life, and he continues to fill her unconscious with his light so that his saving her will be more real to her with each day.

This is the miracle lady's story, but how do we make it come true for ourselves? How do *we* reach the unconscious so that we can be healed and free of our unconscious pain? Obviously, we are not the first to ask these questions and face this problem. Not only many individuals but also every society in the recorded history of civilized mankind has asked this question.

But I find it curious, even devastating, that in modern Western society we have asked and answered this question without a clear picture of the nature and power, indeed the reality of the unconscious. Even in many branches of contemporary clinical psychology—a science which began in the works of Freud and Jung with an active awareness of the reality of the unconscious and its power in the personality of man—and surely in many other institutions of our society, we answer the question of how to change the personality and how to lift the burden of inner pain from man with the ideas of discipline and punishment, and with the inventions of modern science and technology.

All these, however, are tools of the rational mind. Logic, will power, medicine, drugs, etc., while all good, only barely begin to touch the real source of our concern in the unconscious. People need something deeper than the rational to heal the real wound in them. And when we look at the nature of the unconscious we see that the healing agent must be in the nature of an *experience*, for it is a person's experience that has broken him or her in the first place as in the case of the "miracle lady."

But what kind of experience can get deep within a person to touch the memory and the personal and collective unconscious? So many experiences we have each day are shallow in themselves and surely carry no healing power. Only experiences that are deep enough to speak to this dark, mysterious part of people that works on a logic all its own will do—experiences filled with images of hope and healing, experiences weighted with a symbolic nature bringing a person into realities far bigger and more powerful than himself, experiences that are strong enough to undo the destruction of the past and reveal a newer (yet older) and deeper beauty waiting to be found and cherished. With this insight we begin to see a way out of "the human situation" as we have described it.

The Work of Redemption

It is mankind's great and good fortune—our very salvation—that God has seen "the human situation" and decided already to do something about it. Because of the life of Jesus Christ of Nazareth the images, symbols, and experiences that we need to bring abundant life to our brokenness find a firm foundation, an anchor in the reality of a life once lived, a life that was given and sacrificed for all. In other words, the description of "the human situation" as given above is not complete; there is more than just the darkness of the unconscious and the burden of pain it carries. There is light. For God has inserted another truth into the world, or, more correctly speaking, he has asserted the truth of the worthwhileness of creation again, but in an even more powerful way than he stated it "in the beginning." In the life and the mission of Jesus we find a power that grapples with the forces of destruction and death that we find at work in "the human situation." And we find a power that can overcome them.

For Jesus came into the world aware of the totality of mankind's bondage, and he came to free us from every form of bondage. He came to free us spiritually, intellectually, emotionally, and physically. There are many Scriptures that testify to this fact. One is a prophecy foretelling the coming of the Messiah and what he would accomplish for mankind.

While we have looked at it already in an earlier chapter, the beauty and power of this prophecy from the Book of Isaiah bears repeating:

> And yet ours were the sufferings he bore,
> ours the sorrows he carried.
> But we, we thought of him as someone punished,
> struck by God, and brought low.
> Yet he was pierced through for our faults,
> crushed for our sins.
> On him lies a punishment that brings us peace,
> and through his wounds we are healed (Is 53:4-5).

The prophet's vision of the Messiah indicates that his life would bring wholeness to all people, that somehow in his suffering we would find freedom from our suffering. If we could imagine for a moment such a prophecy coming from our lips, we would see that it would be largely inexplicable, surely mysterious and maybe mystical. How could one life change everyone else's so radically? Just how would that work? How could it be? It seems to be nonsense, maybe a desire or a wish, but not a meaningful possibility—not by ordinary, logical ways of thinking. Things just do not happen that way.

Maybe with thoughts similar to these the prophet wrote the words he heard in his heart because he felt they came from God. Or maybe because of his Hebrew background and upbringing he understood them a little better than we can. Still the words of hope that indicate this man, this suffering servant, this Messiah would bring to the human race spiritual renewal ("on him lies a punishment that brings us peace") and spiritual reconciliation ("crushed for our sins"), emotional healing ("ours were the sufferings he bore, ours the sorrows he carried"), and physical wholeness ("through his wounds we are healed"), linger as a promise that this man would be a most unusual and powerful man.

Jesus himself claimed this total view of his life's work as a healing for mankind. It is recorded in the Gospel of Luke that while Jesus was visiting his home town of Nazareth he relied on another similar prophecy to describe his mission:

> The spirit of the Lord has been given to me,
> for he has anointed me.
> He has sent me to bring good news to the poor,
> to proclaim liberty to captives
> and to the blind new sight,
> to set the downtrodden free,
> to proclaim the Lord's year of favor (Lk 4:18).

In this statement it is truly difficult to categorize or limit the effect that Jesus sees his life will have on the entire world. While he indicates clearly an anointing to bring physical healing ("to proclaim . . . to the blind new sight") and to preach the message of God's new friendship with man ("he has sent me to bring good news to the poor"), his words mostly indicate a mission that excludes no problem or limiting situation. Jesus seems to be saying that his life will touch all of life bringing freedom, sight (and insight?), dignity, and the Lord's favor. Surely, after the discussion in this chapter on the bondage to our unconscious psyches in which we all live until we choose to come out of darkness, we can see ourselves in this prophecy and hear Jesus speaking to our needs: "The spirit of the Lord . . . has sent me . . . to proclaim liberty to (you who are) captives. . . ." Jesus' words are announcing a new plan, a new world view, a hope yet unthought of, unimagined, and even unimaginable by man alone. Jesus says his life will change forever "the human situation."

Again in another setting in the Gospel of John, Jesus says the same thing in different words:

> I am the way, the truth and the life.

No one can come to the Father except through me
  (Jn 14:6).

Here Jesus announces that his life and his presence in the
world will bring to all people physical, emotional, intellectual,
and spiritual perfection by bringing them to the Father. He
states that his life is indispensable to anyone who seeks this
wholeness. He says that only in him and through him is unity
with the Father available to mankind, but that *it is readily
available*. Jesus' witness is that he and only he can bring abundant life and freedom into the hearts of mankind, for he unites
men with God.

After Jesus rose, ascended, and sent the Spirit to his
Church, the apostles continued to reflect on the meaning of
Jesus' life in just the same terms. Paul developed his own
language to describe it, but in his many discussions scattered
throughout his letters to the churches about dying to the old
man and rising to new life in baptism we hear references to
this same attitude that Jesus' life has saved us from every
power that could limit us. Peter in his writing, on the other
hand, quotes the ancient sources, among them the prophecies
of Isaiah, to show the meaning of Jesus' mission on earth:

He was bearing our faults in his own body on the cross,
so that we might die to our faults and live for holiness;
through his wounds you have been healed (1 Pt 2:24).

In this verse we see that the faith of Christians from the
earliest times saw Jesus in the same way that he saw
himself—as the suffering Messiah whose life brought healing
and wholeness to all people. Sin had taken hold of mankind
and produced its effects. Immorality, unhappiness, loneliness,
illness, and confusion of intellect and will all abounded because of the power of sin. Jesus healed all these kinds of problems and many more in his ministry, and in his final act of

loving gave up his life to heal every limitation in the lives of human beings.

For it was in his death that Jesus saved all people, including you and me, from sin and its effects. The work of redemption, the Scriptures seem to say, was not only done on the cross but began the evening before in Gethsemane. At that time Jesus, having realized that his giving up his life was to redeem all mankind, united himself to all men spiritually and really. Through prayer—which is communication with God in the depths of self—he became totally open to his own human nature, a nature he shares with every human being. Here we can be assisted by the scheme of the human psyche according to Carl Jung which was presented earlier in this chapter, for it will give us a way of understanding how Christ could be one with all men in his death. For using this approach we can see how Jesus could open himself to the power of the collective unconscious and allow to flow up into his consciousness and his body all the sin, pain, hurt, fear, confusion, and twistedness from every human being who ever had lived, was living, or was to live in times to come. For the collective unconscious is something in which we all participate—as we showed earlier it is roughly equivalent to the concept of human nature—a reality in each human being, a non-physical part of us with energy toward good and evil.

The Gospel of Luke indicates that in Gethsemane Jesus sweat blood, a sign of the excruciating pain he must have endured as he, the Innocent One who never personally experienced sinning, began to feel in all its dark power the evil of human existence. From this moment on until his last breath on the cross when he said, "It is finished," Jesus confronted, experienced, and overpowered the pain of life that we all experience as "the human situation." Thereby he *changed* "the human situation"; he altered it *eternally*. For in overpowering the sin and evil of life he transformed it into positive energy. He took death, faced it, struggled with its power, and made it produce life—an abundant life, a life and a love stronger than death.

In comprehending the vastness of the effects of this one redemptive death, each of us must not forget that in those hours of agony that Jesus experienced to redeem mankind he knew, loved, forgave, and saved each of us *personally*. In entering the collective unconscious and experiencing all sin he experienced *my* sin; in feeling all men's hurt he felt *my* hurt; in forgiving and loving all men—making this sacrifice of the highest order because he saw our need and wanted us saved—he forgave and loved *me*. He has transformed *my* sin into redemption, into life and love. In his death I experienced redemption and freedom in the most personal of ways.

And what a sacrifice it was! Have we ever stopped to consider it? Sometimes maybe we forget what it means that Jesus never himself sinned. He never knew sin in his own life; he never felt the dead feeling it brings to the inner self. He never gave in to a twisted thought that could make him, even for a moment, as we often do for long periods of time, be engulfed in the glamor of evil. What a sensitive man he therefore must have been, open to all his feelings! And all he felt was kindness, compassion, joy. Not once did his life get out of order; there was no taint of pride, selfishness, greed, or lust. If he had ever given in to these attitudes it would have deadened the shock and horror of that Holy Thursday night. But, no, he did not know evil inside him, only outside him; and so, when he began to feel *in* his mind and spirit and body the darkness overtake him, it must have been a truly terrible moment—and it deepened in its horror for hours without relief until the end. Innocence had to be the crucible of our pain so that we could become innocent in God's sight. But what a price to pay! What a dear price for our purchase from death—to have the Innocent One torn apart and ripped as if limb from limb inwardly in the beauty of his soul and outwardly in the torture of his body. Truly, the pain of redeeming us was as much psychological and spiritual as it was physical. And he did it all so that we would not have to be crushed by that evil in a permanent way evermore.

By making us whole in such a complete and everlasting way, Jesus won life in his death. By overcoming and transforming all things that could limit us, he won as a prize for us a simple and honest freedom—a peace with the Father and unity with all creation. In the Nicene Creed we proclaim that he "descended into hell and . . . ascended into heaven." Tradition tells us that after Jesus' death he addressed the souls of all those who had lived before him, preaching to them the Good News of the kingdom of God. In so doing he united all creation in the word of God. Also, personally this doctrine of faith tells me that in knowing me Christ has descended into the depths of my depravation and has ascended into the heights of my sanctification. He knows me in my highest and my lowest, not in two different ways, but in one act of knowing and loving; for through the wholeness won for me by his death he and the Father can accept me just as I am.

This is the victory of resurrection as Jesus experienced it and as I experience it in him—the victory of life and love transforming death, eternally obliterating its power to destroy me in any permanent way. In Christ death becomes life; in him *my* death becomes life. In him the destructive power and darkness of the unconscious which produces what man calls "the human situation" is radically transformed into the possibility of abundant life. It is in this power that Jesus rose from the dead and that we rise with him to an entirely new set of possibilities in life. In the power of divinely-won life we are healed of our infirmities in all areas of our existence, we are transformed into empowered children of God sent to continue his work in the world, and we are allowed to enter his kingdom. Because Jesus is the one who did all this for us, he has become the Lord of life and the Lord of all lives—he is Master because he paid the price for us. And so he has the right to touch any part of our lives, and he wishes to do so to heal us.

For he does not want his redemptive act to be in vain. After winning the victory for us and transforming "the human situation," he does not want us to continue to live as if it all never happened. He wants us to enjoy the fruit of his work— the freedom that is ours through the cross. To live in freedom takes knowledge of the truth of our redemption and faith in Jesus Christ, i.e., a personal relationship with him. And as we relate with Jesus he cannot help but to free us from our problems and our limitations and so make his cross an active part of every day. The wounds that come from darkness he can heal directly in prayer, through the ministry of the Church, and through the love and prayers of individual Christians in whom he also lives. As Jesus reaches out to us and heals our wounds he adds a new and hopeful dimension to "our human situation."

Chapter VI

The Beginning of Inner Healing—Discovering Life in Christ

As beautiful as it is, Jesus' death and resurrection would have little meaning for us if they did not affect each of us personally. If Jesus' Easter mystery were merely a "cosmic truth," an abstraction, or a generality it would be a beautiful thing to behold and it would titillate our emotions, but it would have no lasting meaning or effect for us. Only when I accept the hard fact that Easter is an event that not only happened to Jesus but has also happened to *me*—that Jesus' death and resurrection are not only "cosmic truths" but also are personal truths—only then can the wholeness won for me by Jesus take effect in my personal daily life. Only then will all the Scriptures make sense and I will see that Jesus meant this great gift of abundant life to affect every situation every day.

Many people do not feel the saving efforts of Christ in their day-to-day concerns because they look on the death and resurrection of Christ as only a cosmic truth or an abstraction. Their view of what Jesus has done for us is distant; they accept his saving action as a kindness given by God, but they do not see how it makes any difference as they plod from one problem to another. At best, for these people, Jesus' selfless death is something to think about when times become rough—his love makes them "feel good" in some vague way, and his example gives them courage to go on. But how much these people miss! For in this state of mind Jesus' *resurrection* has little meaning beyond it being the "conclusion to the story." And it is the resurrection of Jesus that allows the whole salvation event to be personal for each human being!

The first time I knew about the resurrection of Jesus was when I was baptized. I did not know about it intellectually, for like many Christians I was baptized as an infant, but spiritually I knew from that moment the resurrected Lord. The verb "to baptize" is not one commonly used by people today. At the time the New Testament was written, however, it was a word in daily usage which religious people of the time appropriated and applied to their need. Commonly speaking, a person two thousand years ago would be said to "baptize" a sponge when he soaked it in water, or to "baptize" a piece of cloth when he put it into a vat of dye. This ordinary use of the word in the ancient world helps us to understand the religious meaning of the word today; for when I was baptized I was immersed in, soaked through with the Holy Spirit, the Spirit who was released upon the world through the work of Christ, the Spirit who teaches me all truth and guides me on my spiritual journey with Christ.

When I was baptized, therefore, I entered the mystery of Christ's resurrection, the event that forever altered dramatically our "human situation," bringing to our fallen human natures hope and wholeness. Consequently, *my* human situation, my human nature was given new possibilities when Jesus came into the human situation as Savior of every part of every human being, and that abundant life was given to me as a personal gift in the event of my baptism.

The effects of my baptism, however, are not mere theological statements or abstractions, but they make a profound difference in each moment of the life I have lived. For, because of baptism, Jesus has been brought into my life and he has walked with me through every experience I have had. Jesus has been with me ministering to me, loving me, caring for me, protecting me, teaching me, healing me at every turn of events I have experienced. This is the effect of the cross reaching out over time to redeem me, here and now. As the Lord of life he *wants* to do this for each human being. "I am the way, the truth, and the life," he said. "No one can come to the Father except through me" (Jn 14:6). And as the Lord of time, the master of all time, the one whom time does not limit, he is *able* to reach across the years from Calvary to today and touch me with his love. "Jesus Christ is the same today as he was yesterday and he will be forever" (Heb 13:8).

I have been baptized into the life of Jesus Christ, and therefore my life has been lived with him and in him; he has lived his life with me and in me. He has always been at my side sharing his very life—which is love, love for me—every minute of every day. Many times the Lord has loved us. We have felt his presence either directly or through the love of people around us, and so we were healed. In the middle of a difficult situation a person was there to help, or a gift of calmness, strength or hope filled us from within, and we were able to recognize the help being given and accept it. These are the good experiences of our lives, the good memories, for we were drawn out of a potentially destructive situation and we received as a gracious gift the light and love of God.

There were other times, however, when life did not flow that smoothly. At these times the painful or destructive situation overwhelmed us, and we did not see or feel the presence of Jesus at our side. Maybe the pain of the situation was too great, maybe things happened so fast that we could not think or pray, maybe we were confused by or torn away from the ones who should have been protecting us, or maybe out of fear we had built up so many defenses to being helped that we actually prevented Jesus from "getting through" to us. Whether one of these was the reason or one of a thousand possible others, only the outcome was important. We were hurt. A part of us was broken, a part of our inner selves. Maybe a part of our psyche was even destroyed in the up-

heaval of the experience. It was not that Jesus was absent—
no, he was there loving us, trying to penetrate the evil that was
surrounding us. But there was something in the situation
and/or something in us that prevented us from seeing his love
and accepting it. And without the love of Jesus evil wins the
victory, at least for the moment.

These are the painful memories in our personal unconscious and the wounded or broken faculties (sub-personalities,
capacities, parts of our inner being) in our spirits. But Jesus
had not stopped having mercy on us; his redemptive suffering,
death, and resurrection had not lost its power to transform
these elements in us. He was at our side loving us in that
situation, and in a sense he is still there, loving us in the same
way, waiting for us finally to accept the love he is giving and
be healed. Even if the event happened years and years ago this
is still true, for time makes no difference to him or to our
spirits. For it is only our consciousness and our bodies that live
in the realm of space and time; our unconscious which is our
spirit lives out of the realm of time, in eternity, as does Jesus
and his Father and the Spirit. This fact may be difficult for us
to imagine, but our difficulty makes it none the less true. The
love of Jesus that would heal everything that hurt and destroyed part of our inner being is hovering over us, and Jesus
stands near us anticipating with gentle joy the moment we will
let his love in.

In the prayer for inner healing, then, all we are doing is
remembering the love that Jesus has already given and accepting it humbly into our hearts where it may comfort and heal
our tired, broken spirits.

The Effects of Unresolved Pain

In the previous chapter we noted that one of the terrible
things about unresolved pain which lives unconsciously in the
memory and personal unconscious is that it festers like a sore,

and it grows by feeding on other pain and destruction until painful or negative memories become negative attitudes, and negative attitudes grow into destructive behavior patterns (sin); these negative behavior patterns, of course, make us feel guilty, and so we begin to protect ourselves with various methods of defense, which also, however, make us more and more lonely. The message of Jesus, the Good News he brings, is that we can be free not only of hurt, but of all that happens in us as a result of hurt, too. He has come to liberate our total selves from the bondage of evil and sin.

Painful memories are bad enough in themselves, but even worse is the limitation they bring into our personal lives, our relationships, and our self-concepts. But whatever limits us, whatever we find obnoxious, unforgivable, or embarrassing about our lives Jesus can heal, and he wants us to know and to believe that he can.

To many people, for example, fear is the controlling factor in life. They become afraid of doing things, of feeling certain emotions, of thinking certain thoughts; soon they become afraid of the future and what it may hold. Consequently, their relationships are affected. If these people have children, they teach their children the same fearful way of living; if the children accept it they are in the same kind of trouble, and if they reject it they often reject their parent as well, along with much fighting and arguing about what is and is not safe to do. With friends and with their spouse these people reveal their fears in conversation and action, often making others uncomfortable and even driving them away. They are difficult to relate with because they are constantly doubting themselves and need so much assurance that they can become a burden to others. Usually fearful people feel to some degree that they are a burden; and often their response is to become afraid even of relationships, because their friends and/or spouse do not seem willing or able to give them what they need, or because they do not enjoy being a burden to them.

The saddest part of a story like this is what something like fear can do to a person's self-concept. People who are controlled by fear feel inferior, unable to manage or cope with the world as well as with themselves and their inner world of emotions. They see themselves as less than others and are anxious to be like them. They often judge that there is something "wrong" with them—an essential part is missing from their emotional world and God must have left it out when he created them.

And so they also begin to doubt God's love for them and to fear God himself. In fearing they are unable to do anything well, they also are afraid that they are unable to please God, and they judge their life as generally unpleasing to him. They see themselves as outside of God's family, as unworthy of joining the intimate circle of his friends, and so they live emotionally distant from him, spending much time and effort (if they come from a religious background) asking him to accept them in some minimal way, or they give up the practice of religion altogether.

The sadness of this pain is that it is felt alone, for most people are too embarrassed to verbalize it in so many words to themselves let alone to share it with another. And so many people go through life never living an abundant life, never feeling the assurance of God being on their side, never having the personal evidence they need to believe that God knows them by name and loves them with strength and gentleness as his own dear child.

The truth is, however, that this is precisely the kind of problem that can be healed by Jesus through what we call the prayer for inner healing. Jesus did not leave us defenseless against such attacks of evil upon our emotions and spirits and relationships. As this person who is controlled by fear has walked through each day of his life, Jesus has been walking with him, loving him and caring for him. His love is still waiting to be accepted and is able to be accepted through prayer.

Very often it is the case with such people that these fears began in childhood, sometimes in a specific experience that brought about great fear in the little child, a scar that would mar his personality by making it defenseless against such fearful experiences in the future. Because Jesus was present with the child in that first fearful experience (although the child who was overwhelmed by the pain of the situation was not aware of his presence), because time does not limit Jesus for he is spiritual and lives in eternity, and because Jesus loves this person as much as he loves the child he once was—which is infinitely—Jesus can gently touch this person's emotions reaching back into time and healing the hurt which came from this experience.

The Effects of Jesus' Healing Love

The transformation that this kind of prayer can make in a person is breathtaking in its total effect. I compare it to striking at the tap root of an old, ugly, unwanted tree: when the tap root is killed and no longer in use the tree must die—it will take some time to see the effects, but we can be certain that the other roots and the rest of the tree will die and decay and fall. The tap root is like that old memory of fear and pain; once it is healed by receiving and accepting the gentle love of Jesus all that has grown from it—negative self-concept, poor relationships, emotional turbulence, feelings of unworthiness to be a child of God—all of these effects too will be healed, not immediately but in time. And the liberation that happens in these people's personalities is a wonder to behold.

Although I have seen many people change in this way, I remember one elderly woman most clearly. She called me at the rectory and asked me to come to her home and pray with her for healing. It is not my custom to go to someone's home to pray, for usually the effort that people make to come to the office or residence of the person who can help them is the first step of their healing—a sign of their willingness to be healed. But I yielded to this lady's request, for her problem was unusual: her fear was that if she left her house something terrible would happen to her. The fear that gripped this lady's heart kept her housebound for weeks and months at a time. If she would leave the house, after a few minutes her anxiety would become unbearable and would take its toll on her heart, her breathing, and her bladder; thus affected, she would retreat to her home, even more afraid of venturing forth again.

After listening to her describe her problem I asked her if she could remember any incidents from her childhood that were extremely fearful. I could see from the look in her eyes that she did not understand what connection there could be, and she was a bit annoyed by this seeming diversion from the subject at hand. It was difficult for her to answer my question with any meaningful memories, until she came upon a memory of being severely punished in school as a little girl. One of the ways this little girl's teacher had of making children behave was by using fear—she would take a misbehaving child to a cellar door, open it, and make the child stare into the cold, dark nothingness. Then she would tell the child that the cellar was filled with bad people, snakes, and spiders, and she would be put down there unless she behaved. At other times she punished children by putting them in a dark closet to scare them into submission.

When the lady told me this story of insensitivity and cruelty from her childhood, I knew that these experiences could be the source of her present fear, at least in part. But I felt there was something more. We talked for a little while longer, and finally the lady recalled some dim memories of traveling as a three-year-old child from Europe to America by steamer. What memories she recalled from that voyage were not good—being alone, feeling helpless, feeling confused. She did not remember her parents comforting her, and it could have been that they actually did not talk too much to the little girl, either thinking that she was too young to be afraid (a common mistake that adults make with children) or being so involved in their worry and anxiety that they did not have time to be with their child and comfort her in her fear.

Without help a little child cannot handle such fear, and so it became an unresolved problem in her, remaining in her unconscious to fester and grow into greater problems in the future. And, of course, as these problems developed later in life, she did not know where they came from and why she did not have that self-confidence other people have. Since she was unconscious or unaware of her own painful experience, she had no way of knowing that, due to a deprivation of love and protection, an important part of her psyche was seriously harmed or even destroyed, leaving her vulnerable to fear and all its corrosive results.

With this story I felt we had come to the heart of the matter. And it was at this point that the lady revealed to me her motive for being healed. All of her life she had wanted to see the Grand Canyon. A friend had offered to take her there, but it had to be soon, and so she needed help fast. Her desire was so innocent and childlike that I was greatly heartened, for I felt that it made her open to God's love for her more fully.

And so we prayed about both experiences. After asking for guidance to see in my own imagination how Jesus was ministering to the hurting little girl who still lived within this elderly woman, I prayed the prayer for inner healing. As I prayed I saw in my imagination how the Lord was at the little girl's side all during that trip across the Atlantic; I saw him gaining her confidence by never leaving her. All she had to do to be relieved of her fear of any strange experience was to look up at him. And often he would remind her of his presence by placing his powerful hand reassuringly on her shoulder. He would answer all of her questions, and if things ever became so confusing or lonely that she had to cry, he was right there to hold her and comfort her until she felt better again.

During this prayer the lady actually did cry as she accepted and received the healing love of the Lord into this part of her heart which had become so tired from bearing the burden of fear for so many years. For in the prayer Jesus did what her mother and father were for whatever reason incapable of doing—loving her enough so that fear would not destroy her self-confidence and her childlike, innocent view of the world.

In a similar fashion we prayed about the incidents in school that had ratified this little girl's fear that the world was not a very pleasant place in which to live. In my imagination and guided by the Spirit I saw that Jesus was with the little girl and her teacher as they looked down those lonely stairs into the cold darkness of the school cellar. I saw Jesus casting the light of his glory down those stairs to show her that there was nothing to fear. I heard him promise her that he would go with her there if the teacher made her go. I saw him lay his hand reassuringly on her shoulder and pray for her that the light of the Holy Spirit would enter all the places in her mind that were in the grip of the darkness of fear.

I also saw Jesus with this little girl as she was sent for a time into the dark closet for a punishment. He held her hand and walked into the closet with her; his light brightened the room and there he comforted her by letting her cry in his arms. He soothed away her loneliness and her fear until she was sure that she was not alone in that place.

Finally, I saw Jesus talk to that teacher in the presence of the little girl, and he told the teacher that she had no right to do these things: these children were entrusted to her for her to educate, not for her to harm. His words were so stern and I could see that he was upset that such a thing was allowed to happen. But his defense of the little girl assured her that she had a powerful friend who would look out after her.

The things this little girl had experienced at the hands of

her teacher had further torn apart her ability to love and affirm herself and to receive these affections from others. When I left her home, the lady assured me that she felt much better, indeed changed.

But of course the proof of such prayers is in the resulting change that may or may not come about in a person's ability to cope with and enjoy life. However, it is not uncommon that a person in my situation never hears about these long-term results from the people we minister to in prayer. That is why I was very pleased months later to receive a postcard from this lady. The picture and the postmark were from the Grand Canyon, and the message was one of profound thanks for helping to make her trip possible. Six months after that I received another letter from her, this time from the Holy Land, and the lady assured me that she was praying for me in all the holy places.

Fear and the problems resulting from it are not the only things that can be healed by Jesus' love. All negative memories, negative attitudes, and negative habits can be healed. Not always does healing mean that the problem will be dramatically torn out of a person's life, but it does mean that Jesus' love will help us find the best resolution possible to the situation that is hurting us. I have seen people healed— i.e., brought by Jesus to a point of freedom so that they could function normally and happily—from many different kinds of emotional, spiritual, and psychosomatic illnesses, including fears and anxieties, anger and hostility, depression, addiction to drugs and alcohol, all kinds of sexual problems, compulsive perfectionism and negative self-image, and neurotic guilt feelings.

These are the feelings, attitudes, and habits within ourselves that *we* want to discard. They become so abominable to us that we do not want to look at them anymore. We become so ashamed of ourselves for having them and we feel so defeated because we have not eliminated them from our lives that our response after a while is to want to throw them away. And we try to do that by forgetting about the problem or at least a part of it—we let it become unconscious. But of course, as we have seen in the last chapter, the unconscious is a real part of us, and when something becomes unconscious we have not thrown it away; but we have used our unconscious as a "garbage dump." We have taken the things we dislike about ourselves the most, judged them as worthless like garbage, and tried to "dump" them by repressing them into a deeper part of ourselves, where they are free to hurt us even more seriously.

Jesus, however, does not see these parts of ourselves in that way at all. For these are parts of *us*, and he loves us, each part of us. He does not love the good part of us more than the bad, the effective more than the ineffective, the whole more than the broken, the sinless more than the guilty, the beautiful more than the ugly. He knows me just as I am, without pretense, and loves me that way; he sees the heights of my holiness and the depths of my degradation and loves it all in one act of loving. For he cannot do anything less than infinitely, even when that means loving something or someone whom *I judge* to be unworthy of his love.

So, when Jesus sees all these parts of me that I reject, he wants to save them, repair them, recreate them, and make them whole. He wants to put the broken me back together again so that I can reclaim myself, and begin to live a full life with my self made whole in his love, and cease living a half-life with only the half of myself that I judge as acceptable. And in this way Jesus makes these parts of me new and he makes *me* new, so that I can love myself as much as he loves me. In this way I enter his will, I enter the world of his love, I enter the kingdom of God.

It is very much like what happened to the woman who came into the feast of Simon the Pharisee to anoint Jesus' feet and dry them with her hair (Lk 7:36-50). Simon sat there watching everything critically and said to himself, "If this man were a prophet, he would know who this woman is that is touching him and what a bad name she has." But the fact was that Jesus *did* know who this woman was—who she *really* was in the eyes of God—for he saw deeply inside her to the real person there. He saw the person beneath the mask of hurt, sin, and self-degradation that other people had put on her and that she had accepted over the years of her life. And as he saw that person he loved her and allowed her to act as she was always meant to act—as a child of God. For Jesus was present when the Father created her and he saw and loved her from the first. So Jesus saw the saint within the sinner and loved that saint within so that she could come out and show the world that this was her true nature.

Jesus does the same for you and me. He was with us when we were created in our Father's hands as a pure spirit and loved us completely then. He was with us when that spirit was joined with our bodies in our mother's womb and has remained with us ever since, knowing and loving who we really are. And he is not waiting to come to me until I am perfect, but, knowing who I really am and loving that person deep within, he is most anxious to take from me all that encumbers my real self from expressing its best qualities. For he enjoys seeing me happy, and when I am happy I can give him my best praise.

This is the reason, then, that every person needs inner healing; for everyone has sinned and everyone has been hurt by others in their lives; therefore, everyone needs to be transformed in Christ. Inner healing is the way that we begin to feel the effects of Christ's saving love within us. As such, inner healing itself is nothing new, for as long as men and women have preached the crucified Lord who has saved us from our sins, Christians have experienced some form of inner healing or inner transformation—some, of course, to a greater extent than others. What may be news to many Christians, however—and I believe it is *Good News*, an integral element of the Gospel preached by Jesus, Paul, and the apostles—is that we can pray for specific parts of our personalities and spirits to receive the love of Jesus to transform them in dramatically liberating ways, so that we can begin to taste the glory of the children of God right now.

The Need for Jesus' Healing Love

I don't believe there is a person alive who is honest with himself who will deny his need of such liberation through love. The beautiful counterpart to that need in all of us is that Jesus is waiting to come into our hearts with his love to liberate us. And it is my experience that as we present each part, each experience of our lives to the Lord to be touched by his love, there is nothing too small for Jesus to be concerned about and nothing too big, ugly or complex for him to handle. He is simply waiting to be our servant and wash away whatever hurt is limiting us from being whole, so that we can learn from him how to open our lives to being each other's servants, allowing him to minister to others through us. "If I do not wash you, you can have nothing in common with me," Jesus said to Peter at the Last Supper (Jn 13:8), and he says it to each of us as well. Unless we allow him to be our servant and to heal our deep inner hurting selves, we will not be able to share his abundant life with him or with others.

What are the kinds of experiences that need healing love to touch them and make them whole? We have already seen many examples in this book of the love of Jesus touching people in different life situations to bring them freedom; and in general we can say that any time in our life when we have experienced sin or the effects of sin is a time that needs the love of Jesus brought into it to make it whole. The circumstances of our conception and our heredity, the time we spent in the womb, and the experience of birth—all may have been times of hurt or sin that are still affecting us today. For example, if accidents happened to us, if our life was attacked, if we were abandoned or adopted as I was, if our parents had a strongly negative experience during this time like a divorce or a death in the family, if our parents had negative feelings about the fact that we were to be born, or if any other negative experiences happened that involved the people who were supposed to be protecting us with love and care, these experiences are imprinted within us and affect our feelings, attitudes toward life, and behavior even today. These experiences need the love of Jesus to heal them and free us.

All the negative experiences we had with our mothers, fathers, and family need the healing love of Jesus—all the mistakes our parents made in raising us, the times their problems so overwhelmed them that they could not take care of us in the way that they wanted to, any cruelty we may have experienced from them or other family members, any time we felt abandoned because they deserted us or the family or due to diseases or their death, any argumentative, uncommunicative, or overdependent elements in our relationship with them. For many of us our experiences in school with teachers and with classmates are sources of great hurt in us affecting our present behavior—Jesus wants to take the hurt from the memory so that it cannot limit us anymore. Any sudden or dramatic change in a child's life will affect that child far more deeply than most adults are sensitive to, so experiences of death, even—and especially, in the case of many children— the death or loss of a pet, accidents the child may suffer, or the experience of the family moving to a new location—all may leave deep scars that time alone will not so much heal as cover and that will need the love of Jesus to be totally healed.

Very often childhood does not adequately prepare a person for adult life, especially in the area of self-confidence and ego development. So many experiences that happen to children can shatter their concept of themselves and thus weaken them emotionally for the responsibilities and tasks of adult-hood. A lady once came to me in this state, and she expressed her weakness in an extremely nervous temperament, in an inability to make decisions, and in physical nervous disorders. At the time I met her she was taking much medication to calm her, but it was no longer having much effect. She would spend hours each day lying down trying to compose herself, some-times after an argument but also at times in reaction to an inner anxiety that made her afraid to face even a normal day.

I began to see her weekly and to pray with her. During each of the fourteen sessions we had, before we prayed, of course, she would talk with me about her problems and feelings, and these would be the subject of our prayers. We started with her present situation and worked backward in time. We talked and prayed about her relationship with her six children and her feelings about how they treated her and how she treated them; we prayed about her relationship with her husband who was not sensitive to her emotional and physical problems; we prayed about her nervousness itself. But soon we talked about her childhood, and there we found the source of many of her difficulties. Because she was unaware of the effect that childhood experiences can have on adult life, she had dismissed these experiences as sad memories to be forgot-ten, and they were difficult to bring forth again.

But what we found was a not too untypical situation. She was one of the middle children in a poor family of nine. Her father was an alcoholic and one day deserted the family. Her mother then had to work to support her children. With the children left in the care of the eldest, the "law of the jungle" prevailed and the bigger and stronger ones lorded it over the smaller and weaker ones. With no adults around who had the time to pay attention to the children, they lived without direc-tion, without acceptance and approval, and without being taught the qualities a mature adult is expected to have. This little girl, living in the midst of a virtual emotional maelstrom, grew up without a sense of "self" as unique and valuable.

It is not uncommon that a person like this, whose main attitude toward life is fear and anxiety, is attracted to a spouse who seems to be an emotional rock, but who indeed is only insensitive and incapable of dealing with his or her mate's insecurities. And so when, at an early age, this woman found her "rock" and married him and he began to make decisions impervious to her needs, her inner emotional turmoil only grew. With each child came an added responsibility, a deeper sense of loneliness, and a greater awareness that she had been abandoned and had not been loved for herself; for her husband never helped in guiding, disciplining, and caring for their children. Finally her body began to express her anxiety and anger; and since the problem was mainly emotional, drugs could only be a partial and incomplete answer to the problems of her life.

In helping this woman, it was not important to uncover specific situations of hurt as much as it was necessary to look at the relationships that were important to her—the quality of those relationships and her feelings about them—and to admit the depth of hurt that was there because of her father's abandonment, her mother's seeming lack of concern for the problems of each child, and her older siblings' dominance of her. All of these feelings did not come out of her unconscious at once, of course; but as each feeling came forth, we prayed that she would be able to join Jesus in forgiving each person who hurt her and to accept Jesus' comfort and love to heal her own pain.

As this lady began to let Jesus work in her psyche, light came into her eyes, the confused and depressed tone lifted from her voice, and she began to be able to cope with each day's concerns. She allowed Jesus to give her a reason to live a full life again and resolved not to retreat to her bedroom in the midst of trouble but rather to believe that Jesus was with her strengthening her every step of the way. She has stopped taking most of her medication and, with a renewed relationship with Jesus which she has learned to nurture by having a healthy spiritual life, with the support of a local prayer group, and with a new sense of her own worth and value as a person, she is living a new and abundant life, a life in Christ. Not that everything is perfect: her husband has not changed much and still does little to support her, and once in a while she will have a bout with one of her children or with a neighbor that will threaten her new freedom. But she is able to live a productive life, to feel worth something, to find at least some happiness. And she is truly grateful for what Christ has given her spiritually in his relationship with her, for she "has chosen the better part; it is not to be taken from her" (Lk 12:42).

These blessings came to this woman because of the death and resurrection of Christ which she first participated in through her own baptism. The same is true for all of us. As we begin to accept through faith the personal relationship we have with Christ because he is alive, as we begin to accept all that he has done for us, we feel the effects of his healing love in the very fabric of our lives. Our free will allows him to enter us personally and he can tear down the fortress of sin and the walls of loneliness and desperation. He can heal the broken limbs and open wounds of pain and make us whole and free.

We need him. Our "human situation" demands it. No one else can handle problems of that magnitude. No one else has been given the power to heal in such a way; no one else has the gentleness to touch my wounds in a way that will not hurt even more; no one else cares about me enough to give me as much time as I need without limit; no one else knows me well enough to decide what can be healed because it is really me and what has to be discarded because it is merely a mask I have put on—no one but Jesus.

In seeing our need clearly and in seeing Jesus' loving power to heal us, the sense of our own unworthiness—a feeling many people share—sinks into the background. How often we allow our own feelings of unworthiness to prevent us from finding the love we need! It may be one of the most common problems of humankind today. For many people have an inner anxiety that the good things of life, even spiritual life, are meant for everyone else but them.

Only the Gospel can dismiss that cloud of unworthiness from over our head. For that is the Good News that the Gospel story tells: once we *were* unworthy but we no longer are, not because of anything we have done, but because of something *God* has done. He accomplished this gracious deed of his own free will; he gave us a gift. Jesus Christ is his gift to us, and by his becoming man our unworthy human natures were *made worthy*, were redeemed, were made whole. This message is the essence of the Gospel, and especially as we come to the decision whether or not to accept Jesus' saving love through inner healing, we must hold fast to this truth. If we conclude our investigation of inner healing by saying, "That's very nice for everyone else, but it's not for me because I'm not good enough," then we have nullified everything with one stroke. We nullify God's efforts to save us; we nullify the very meaning of our own lives, i.e., Jesus' love for us.

Jesus does not come to us as a great important person for whom we could in theory not be good enough. He never presented himself that way. Rather, he is the humblest of all beings. He emptied himself as the Son of God, putting aside his divinity so that he could be "a man like us in all things but sin" (*The Roman Missal*, Eucharistic Prayer IV); he lived at a time when the Jewish people were a politically downtrodden race; he was born into a poor family and not a wealthy or even middle-class one; when he was born he did not even have a home; he worked hard as a common man; as a rabbi he lived without a place to lay his head; he died a criminal.

Surely no one on this earth has to look up to him in any human sense. He wanted it that way. He and his Father planned it that way so that no one would ever feel unworthy in his presence. He does not come to us at the highest social level to make us feel inferior; rather he comes to us at the lowest level so that, no matter who we are, what our background is, or what we have done we can feel comfortable with him.

Furthermore, he continues to describe himself as our servant, and he comes to us as a helper. Maybe the best modern image I have heard to describe him is "the junk collector." He takes our garbage and hauls it away for us; but the really precious things that we want to throw away because they are dirty or broken he finds, saves, repairs, and then he returns them to us. The image of Jesus, his hands dirty with the work of the day, dressed in poor and ragged clothing, smiling and whistling a happy song, stopping to talk with everyone, especially little children, at first may be disconcerting, but finally it warms our hearts with an assurance that Jesus is working at our side at the business of life.

Who could be so powerful as to transform every human life and yet accomplish such a huge task in the humblest of ways? No one but Jesus. It is *in* his humility, then, that he becomes the most important being and the one most honored by his Father. This means that he never loses his humility as he takes on the task of bringing all men to himself and giving over all creation to his Father. Because he always will be humble we do not have to be afraid of his power.

This is the mystery of Christ. The gift of inner transformation, the healing of the inner person, centers around the mystery of him who "emptied himself to assume the condition of a slave" (Phil 2:7), and yet is "first in every way, because God wanted all perfection to be found in him and all things to be reconciled through him and for him" (Col 1:18b-19). As we enter this mystery more fully, accepting the power and the humility of Christ, allowing ourselves to know him and his personality, and trying to live in the same way he does, we will put aside our mask of unworthiness and begin to have a relationship with him.

As we allow him to communicate his feelings for us and his personal knowledge of and acceptance of us, as we learn more about who Jesus really is and how he works in our world, the mystery of our own healing begins to unfold. Our "human situation" is laid bare and the only answer to it that works comes clear. Then all the knots of confusion begin to untangle, for in the presence of Jesus all things become simple and whole.

Chapter VII
The Fulfillment of Inner Healing—
Forgiveness and Love

When we have looked squarely at "the human situation" and when we look at the solution which God has offered to the world for this problem, i.e., Jesus Christ and our chance to live in and through him, then we are beginning to view life through God's eyes. We are developing a world-view very different from that of secular mankind, whether we are influenced by Western or Eastern culture. The Christian point of view is unique and special because in Christ all of mankind's limitations can be overcome through faith, hope, and love.

But merely taking on God's point of view does not change us and bring us the healing we seek. We must become involved. If we choose to *experience* God's way of life, we find a way to be open to changing our present way of life. As Jesus led people along this road from the world into the kingdom of God, he said that the first step into the kingdom was forgiveness. Indeed, then, forgiveness is also often the first step in inner healing. If we want to become whole and holy, we must learn about forgiveness, giving and receiving it.

Holiness is completeness, soundness, healthiness of spirit. A holy person is one who lives in right order with God and with other human beings; he is a person into whom grace can flow freely from God and through whom grace can flow unimpeded to others. To be this kind of person we need to be healed of the inner hurts that cause us to block the flow of grace from God to us and to others, and to be healed we need to experience forgiveness. "Grant pardon, and you will be pardoned," Jesus said (Lk 6:37).

Forgiveness, then, is often the first step to wholeness, to light penetrating our unconscious which has been darkened by sin and hurt. We can look at the experience of forgiveness under three aspects: first, receiving forgiveness for past sins and faults; second, seeking forgiveness for the sinfulness still present in our lives; and third, giving forgiveness to everyone who has ever hurt us.

Receiving Forgiveness for Past Sin

First, we are called upon to receive forgiveness for the sins of our past for which we are sorry and for our failures. This seems at first to be an easy task until we realize how often each of us refuses this simple, gratuitous gift. We can refuse the great experience of God forgiving us for many reasons: maybe we were too proud to admit we were wrong in the first place; maybe we found it impossible to believe that God could be so merciful to us; maybe our sin made us so ashamed we have not been able to look at it squarely enough to ask forgiveness for it. For whatever reason many people walk around in life with a burden of guilt that makes them feel depressed, confused, and unworthy; yet all they need do to drop that burden is go to God with their guilt and say with humility and sincerity, "I'm sorry." Many times Jesus assured us that our Father is anxiously awaiting our return home so that he can forgive us completely, and so that we can feel like his beloved son or daughter again.

Sometimes a failure to believe in God's complete forgiveness is caused by or results in a failure to forgive ourselves as well. A lady once approached her minister to confess a sin which weighed heavily on her conscience. "I don't know what to do, Father," she said. "I've asked God to forgive me for this sin a thousand times, but my guilt remains as heavy as it first was months ago." But knowingly the priest replied, "My friend, the Lord forgave you the first time you asked him to; your problem is that you have asked his forgiveness nine hundred and ninety-nine times too many."

The person who has a problem in receiving God's forgiveness really has a prior problem, for he has forgotten what it means to be a child of God. When we listen with openness to the way God views us because we are his children we find it difficult to feel unforgiven. For example, St. Paul tells us: "He has reconciled you. . . . Now you are able to appear before him holy, pure, and blameless" (Col 1:22); and again he says: "He has overridden the Law, and cancelled every record of the debt that we had to pay; he has done away with it by nailing it to the cross" (Col 2:14). God has taken us into his own family, not because of anything we have done, but because of his love for us. And his love is always faithful. It is not like human love which varies with moods and situations and which reacts more strongly to some people than to others. And as members of his family God has pronounced us free, forgiven, blameless. He sees us as beautiful and spotless, holy and pure.

In other words, we do not have to be afraid to go to him aware of our sin, because before we can even begin to apologize he sees the repentance in our heart and says, "My child, how beautiful you are! How good it is to have you near me! I love you. Be free."

And so when sins of the past begin to condemn us and trouble us, we can turn to God our Father and to Jesus Christ so that their love will once and for all set us free. We do this by first of all admitting that what we did was sinful and then claiming our freedom as children of God and letting our sins go. We may pray a prayer of inner healing, imagining ourselves at the foot of the cross with the black, ugly mess of sin in our hands and leaving it there to be touched by the blood of

Jesus. We may imagine our sin as chains binding us which Jesus rips from us setting us free. We may visualize our shame and depression in images, seeing ourselves surrounded by darkness reaching to the Lord who shines on us as the bright light of day filling us with that light that is him. We may imaginatively recreate the circumstances of which we are ashamed but also see Jesus there loving us even when we were in the midst of our sin. We may ask Jesus to touch gently our spirits which we have wounded and disfigured with sin and, just as he healed the broken and withered bodies of many, to heal our inner selves that we may be beautiful and strong again, so that we might serve him better.

But however we pray it is important to continue to pray until we *experience* God's forgiveness for our sins. That he has already forgiven them is a fact—the fact of his death on the cross. So if we do not feel that forgiveness after feeling our sorrow, the resistance is in us and not in him. He is most anxious to help us feel forgiven, for no guilt-ridden person can be an effective witness of his love. And once we have asked in a situation as delicate as this, it is best not to ask again but rather to take the more positive stance of thanking God for his forgiveness as it comes. For continuous asking may be in reality giving in to a weakness in faith that God will not forgive. Many people have a deep fear within them that God can forgive anyone but them; whether this fear comes from pride or from an extremely low self-image, we cannot give in to it, for it can only be destructive. We must acknowledge the fear as real and then present it to the Lord, for "fear is driven out by perfect love" (1 Jn 4:18), and Jesus' perfect love casts out all fear. Filled with that love, we will be able to trust the Lord's promise: "I will never call their sins to mind, or their offenses" (Heb 10:17).

Seeking Forgiveness for Present Sin

After we have accepted the truth that God has already and graciously forgiven the sin in our past, it will be less difficult to seek out his forgiveness for the sin that still controls our lives. That sin would not still be in us if we did not allow and sometimes even want it. Thus when we face that sin squarely we face a difficult decision: Which do we want more, an abundant life in the freedom that only God can give or the temporary pleasure of our sin? For to the extent we want the sin that is in our lives we are not open to the regenerating power of God. Seeking the abundant life of God through healing, then, asks of me a decision and a commitment.

Part of the problem of asking forgiveness for our sin is that many people in modern society have lost their sense of conscience. The distinction between right and wrong has become progressively more vague in our society. This kind of confusion leads people on a downward spiral of amorality, for as the difference between right and wrong becomes cloudy it takes more effort to ascertain what is the right thing to do. Feeling morally confused we lose sight of those harbor lights of guidance that can help us find our way and often we lose the will to find them. It seems easier and more agreeable to live by our own rules which we often establish on the basis of our own narrow experience. If from this point of view very little seems sinful and wrong, then we have very little for which to ask forgiveness.

The fact is, however, that there are some objective standards of right and wrong and some time-tested guidelines for how to live a godly and productive life. Running from these facts does not change them, and choosing not to acknowledge them makes them no less true. And because these are facts our lives will not be happy or fulfilled until we live according to them. Not doing so only destroys us, corroding our inner selves.

It is in yielding to God and to his word, the Bible, that we find the truth which will make our lives happy. In going back to the Bible we can find the principles upon which to base our lives. And yet, as we discover the principles of a good life, we can never apply them with condemnation, for "those who are in Christ Jesus are not condemned" (Rom 8:1). Rather, compassion is the quality that emulates God's stance toward us, and so we should develop it as we begin to live our lives according to the dignified standards that God has for his children. What the Lord desires from us, we must remember, is a change of heart, not once but often. Real repentance is not loving the Law in itself or obeying it for its own sake, but rather turning toward a loving God to accept his forgiveness and changing our ways out of gratitude for his mercy.

When we choose to remain only vaguely aware of what is sinful, all we are doing is repressing our guilt into our unconscious to control us in just the same way as unconscious hurt can take over so much of our lives. But when we admit our sin simply and humbly, are sorrowful, and seek forgiveness, we, with the power of Christ surging through us, become masters of sin and we are set free.

Forgiveness to Others

It is a truism to say that a person cannot give that which he does not possess. That is the reason it is essential that we know about, receive, and seek God's forgiveness in as total a way as possible: for once we are sure we possess God's forgiveness we will be able to turn to our neighbor and forgive him his wrongdoing against us. To have mercy, to forgive, to pardon others their faults is essential to living a Christian life, an abundant life.

Many people do not know *how* to forgive, however, for they were never taught; maybe all they ever knew as children was heavy demands, strict rules, high standards, and guilt heaped upon them if they did not measure up. If that was their situation they need to feel God's forgiveness of them to free up their heart enough to have mercy on another. They may even need his forgiveness to give them their first model of forgiving love. But once the process is started it is usually self-perpetuating: forgiveness received leads to forgiveness given, which leads to forgiveness received at even a deeper level. As Jesus said, "Be compassionate as your Father is compassionate. Do not judge, and you will not be judged yourselves; do not condemn, and you will not be condemned yourselves; grant pardon, and you will be pardoned. Give, and there will be gifts for you: a full measure, pressed down, shaken together, and running over, will be poured into your lap; because the amount you measure out is the amount you will be given back" (Lk 6:36-38).

When one assembles all the passages in Scripture on the importance of giving mercy and forgiveness, the evidence is quite astounding. Surely this principle is among the most important if not *the* most important in the New Testament. Among these passages, besides the one quoted above, are the Beatitudes, which are the code of life in the kingdom of God (Mt 5:1-12), and the Our Father (Mt 6:7-15), two of the most important teachings of Jesus' life; his words from the cross (Lk 23:34); his explanation of how to pray effectively (Mk 11:20-25); his answer to Peter (Mt 18:21-22); the story of the woman caught in adultery (Jn 8:1-11); the story of the woman who washed his feet with her tears (Lk 7:36-50); and many parables such as the Good Samaritan (Lk 10:29-37), the Lost Sheep (Lk 15:4-7), the Lost Drachma (Lk 15:8-10), the Prodigal Son (Lk 15:11-32), and the Unforgiving Debtor (Mt 18:23-35).

Why is forgiving others so important? Because it frees the spirit to receive, pray, love, and be healed. I remember a most important experience when I learned this truth the hard way. I had come to a point in my life when I wanted to give myself

completely over to God by asking the Holy Spirit to fill me
with himself and his gifts and to take over my life. Charisma-
tics and Pentecostals call this the baptism in the Spirit or the
release of the Holy Spirit. It was an important decision I was
making, and I placed great weight upon it, for I had never
before handed my life over to anyone in any way. I was told
that when I made this prayer sincerely I could expect to have
an experience of the Holy Spirit giving me his joy and peace.
So I was prepared for the day in every way but one—one to
which I was blind. I prayed long and hard each day for a
week; I tried to purify my motives to make them other-
centered rather than self-centered; I fasted; but I did not look
at my life and see where I needed to forgive and be forgiven.

It was not that God did not point out this need in my life;
one day in prayer I spontaneously opened my Bible to the
fourth chapter of the Letter of James which begins "Where do
all these wars and battles between yourselves first start?"
However, I was blind to the warning there that my life was
marred with arguments with two fellow workers whom I
judged and condemned severely. I had never forgiven them
their faults, and this attitude had caused arguments for which
I also needed their forgiveness. Blindly I continued through
my week, looking forward to the day when God would fill me,
but not realizing that I was unprepared to receive him.

When the day came, I prayed, and people prayed with
me, but no interior experience of God happened. I was
crushed in despair. "Is there no way I can find God again?" I
cried to myself. That night I went to bed in tears, I woke up
the next morning in tears. That day happened to be Palm
Sunday, and as I dressed and prepared for Mass my heart was
as heavy as it could be.

But at Mass a light began to flicker. I listened to the
Gospel of the crucifixion of our Lord, and something within
me began to stir. The soldiers . . . Jesus . . . condemned . . .
crucified . . . all these images whirled around in my head. I

wanted to go somewhere and think things through; since it was early in the morning I thought of going out to a snack shop for breakfast alone. As I sat there thinking, the inspiration of the Spirit came upon me—I was like the soldiers, for I was condemning two men and "crucifying" them with my judgments and constant bitterness. In preparation for the release of the Spirit I had been told that the Holy Spirit cannot fill a heart that is already filled with resentments, for the two are incompatible. Then and there I admitted my sin of self-righteousness, judging others, resentment, bitterness, and arguing for my own gain. And then and there, amid the plastic flowers and fake-wood paneling of a snack shop, I cried the tears of release as I was freed of my burden of sin and was allowed to be the real person God had made me to be. I forgave my brothers in Christ in my heart at that moment, and sought their forgiveness personally during the next two days.

Forgiveness frees. That is the reason Jesus urges us so emphatically to forgive. And total forgiveness frees totally. That is the reason Jesus does not qualify his statements on forgiveness, for he loves us enough to want us to find total freedom to be our real selves.

Therefore, Jesus does not tell us that we have to forgive only the big things or that we can forgive only the little things. He does not say to us that you must forgive some people but not others, for example, "You don't have to forgive your parents," or "You don't have to forgive the person who stole your money." He merely says, "Forgive. Forgive and know the peace which the world cannot give."

And so it is important, as soon as we realize our need to forgive, to walk through our life in our memory and to forgive all the people who ever hurt us, whether or not they are now alive or dead, whether the hurt they caused was great or small, whether or not I can remember their names. I must come simply and humbly to forgive everyone, from my parents to the child who embarrassed me in front of my classmates, from the teacher who did not understand me and made my life difficult to the friend who snubbed me, from the spouse who hurt me intimately to the business associate who cheated me. Also and especially, if I have felt that God cheated or hurt me—for example, in the death of a loved one, or because of my vocation—I must forgive him too. Otherwise, my relationship with him will never be free.

While all this is necessary and must be done, it all does not have to—indeed, it cannot—happen in one day. What the Lord is looking for is a sign of openness and a sincere promise to work on each memory until I have totally forgiven. At the beginning, to want to forgive is enough; even to *want* to want to forgive is enough when the hurt seems too big to tackle all at once. But what I am aiming for is total forgiveness which will open me up to total wholeness.

How To Forgive

What the best way to forgive may be is a topic of much discussion. From my point of view the best way—because it is the safest way in that it protects the one we are forgiving—is through prayer. Many feel the need to forgive another face-to-face, but often this feeling can be a subtle mask for the desire to hurt others by telling them how much they hurt us. This is not forgiveness; it is retribution, paying back evil with evil instead of evil with good as the Lord urges us. What good would it do, for example, to hunt down a grammar school teacher and tell her what her insensitivity did to me? I would only lay a burden of guilt on her in order to absolve her. In this way I only nurture my pride.

If we forgive another in our heart in prayer, our forgiveness is no less real, and we save the other person the embarrassment of seeing the effects of his faults displayed before him. (On the other hand, when *we* are *seeking* forgiveness from another, then we go to him face-to-face if at all possible; and in our humbling we will be lifted up.) We can pray the prayer of forgiveness most realistically in the same way we pray for other kinds of healing—by using our imagination to visualize the person and maybe also to re-enact the situation in which we were hurt, to see the Lord forgiving the person, to feel him healing us of the hurt that we experienced, and to unite ourselves with his forgiving love, letting his infinite forgiveness flow through us.

This last is an important point, for if I do not forgive with the forgiveness of Christ, then what I do is worth little. For the forgiveness which comes from my heart alone cannot help being partial and incomplete. Only Christ's forgiveness is total and sets me totally free. Therefore, another excellent way to pray to forgive another is to see ourselves and the one we need to forgive both standing side by side at the foot of the cross, to see how Jesus loves us both equally and infinitely, and to accept the truth that Jesus suffered and died for both of us equally because both of us have sinned.

Sometimes when people hear this message they become anxious because they feel they cannot forgive certain things they have experienced. Immediately they focus in on the most difficult situation in their life and feel defeated before they start. This attitude, however, is no help to anyone as they begin to share Christ's way of treating others; it is also no help to them in their desire for healing. This attitude is, on the other hand, a sign of how hard people can be on themselves, how demanding they are, and how poor their self-image is.

While forgiving those who have hurt us is often the first step to healing, many other times it is the second, and the first in these cases would be a request that Jesus heal the hurt enough so that we are free to forgive it. For sometimes our desire to hold on to a resentment is a desire to "get back" at the person who hurt us; if we find ourselves in this situation we can ask Jesus to heal that deep-seated bitterness so that we no longer will have a need to retaliate evil for evil, and then we will be free to forgive.

All of this takes time. Important things often do take time—much time. Jesus is aware of this truth and is willing to give us the time it takes to forgive fully and freely. Most often, at the beginning of this journey of healing and forgiveness, human beings do not have the same attitude toward it as Jesus does: either they do not want to devote adequate time and effort to this project, not seeing its value and not admitting their own need; or they want it done, but immediately, becoming impatient with themselves and anxious over the situation. If we find ourselves with either of these attitudes we know that we are not just "out in left field," we are in "another ball park," for Jesus "plays the game of life" by entirely different rules. First, we must calm ourselves and try to look at the project from his point of view.

Jesus' point of view is a love for us that is both firm and gentle. So, while he wants us on one road, not diverting from his way, he guides us gently. And in his gentleness he teaches the principles of forgiveness:

1. Receive forgiveness so that you can give it.

2. Seek forgiveness for your own sins so that you will be sensitive to others' shame over their sins against you.

3. In the beginning, to want to forgive is enough.

4. Do not necessarily begin by trying to forgive the biggest hurt of your life; if necessary, build up to it.

5. Forgive everything, big and small, but take the time to forgive fully and freely.

6. Forgive with the forgiveness of Christ; do not think the forgiveness you need to give must come from you alone.

7. Forgive, in prayer, the hurt others caused you; seek forgiveness face-to-face for the hurt you caused them.

8. Be gentle with yourself as Christ is gentle with you; be sensitive to your own needs and learn to love yourself.

When we forgive or are forgiven, something wondrous

happens: things and people become real again. For sin is a mask of unreality—it is a creature not from God but from man, and as such it will not live into eternity. Sin is the "self" that *we* create to hide the real self that God has made. Therefore, when we are forgiven God takes off *our* mask and allows us to be the creatures he has made us to be—simple, loving, sensitive, creative, relational beings. When we forgive others, and even when we forgive God, a similar thing happens. For, in holding resentments, we place a mask over another in our own mind. We do not see that person in his reality, for we are focusing in on one element of our relationship with him and emphasizing it out of proportion to the rest. In forgiving another we allow God to take the mask from our eyes and we see in our former enemy our own brother or sister.

Forgiveness, then, makes the object of forgiveness real. This is one of the greatest reasons we need to become masters at forgiving. When we accept or give forgiveness, we are cooperating with the power of Jesus on the cross, making the world "real" again, relieving it of the encumbrance of sin which had hidden its beauty and reality by deforming it. As the Holy Spirit moves in our hearts to accept and give forgiveness, he heals that deformity so that we can be real to God and the world, and God and the world can be real to us.

When forgiveness becomes so much a part of us that it is not a difficult act but a habit, we find ourselves in a world we can enjoy, we find ourselves in situations that can touch us and change us, we find ourselves in relationships in which we can feel like a real human being giving and receiving love. In other words, forgiveness destroys our personal prison of loneliness and despair, for in forgiveness we have taken close to our own hearts the attitude and person of Christ, and Christ then can lead us into community with self (knowing ourselves and the different parts of ourselves, communication with our unconscious), with others (friendships, church, associations of mutual growth), and with the three Persons of God (discerning his actions in our lives and in the world, prayer and meditation, living our life in him).

Jesus spoke to Peter about the necessity of making forgiveness a habit (Mt 18:21-22; Lk 17:3-4). Peter asked him, "Lord, how often must I forgive my brother if he wrongs me? Seven times a day?" And Jesus said to him, "Oh, no, Peter, you have it all wrong; not seven times a day, but seventy times seven times if necessary." To the Hebrew, seven was a mystical number and it denoted perfection. Jesus was telling Peter that he was to forgive exactly the number of times that he was wronged—that he was not allowed to hold back forgiveness for whatever reason.

But once, just for the fun of it, I figured out mathematically what seventy times seven times a day would yield: the answer is once every two minutes and fifty-six seconds, and that is on a basis of twenty-four hours without time for sleeping. That is how often we are to forgive if it is necessary and I think we all can say that we have had some days on which it *was* necessary. For what can heal a broken relationship except forgiveness? It is the only glue that works. When a relationship breaks down we face a choice between hurt and loneliness on one side and forgiveness and love on the other.

The only remedy for inner pain, then, is God's love. Forgiveness is one way of participating in it, and an important way, but at other times the only answer to the pain of life is a direct outpouring of God's love for us. His perfect love is the power of healing. Sometimes the only thing that will comfort and empower me is the experience of someone knowing me just as I am—the good and bad of it all—and loving me just that way. Of course, the only one who can do that is Jesus.

It is as if he finds me along the road of life. I am crippled, withered, disfigured; maybe I am severely wounded, and I am bleeding and losing life. He would not think of walking by. Rather he stops, takes me into his arms, and gently comforts me. With great compassion and tenderness he washes my wounds and bandages them. He nourishes me; he rests and waits with me until I am able to move again. And then very carefully he leads me down the road and takes me to his Father.

As I approach the Father's presence I feel something I have never felt before—a love that is passionate and overwhelming, and I know it is for me. His feelings for me are so strong that I can hardly look at him. Surely he loves me more than I love myself. For he is seeing his own creation and is loving a unique creature that he has taken much time and care to form. He looks at me and sees his very own child—a kinsman, a son, one who is marked to inherit all that he has.

And Jesus says to his Father, "Look, Father, I have brought Ted to you. I found him along the road and he was in such bad straits that I had to help. I know he doesn't look all that good at the moment, for he's been hurt pretty badly. But I was wondering, Father, if you could help him too. Could you accept a broken son of yours to make him whole again?"

And the Father says, "Why, my Son, of course I can. He is my very own. How could I refuse him and why would I want to? He is my special child. And, yes, he does look quite broken from his journey, my Son, but I remember one time when you were even more broken than that. That day on Calvary you bore all the brokenness of humanity, and I still accepted you then. No, there's no problem loving him, especially because you have brought him to me, and I love both of you very much. I can already see some of the effects that your relationship has had on Ted, and that makes me love him over and over again. Yes, I accept him. Let us give him our special gift."

So, the Father and the Son give me their Spirit—their very own life and love, the most intimate communion of love in the universe. And the Spirit cleanses me, purifies me. Then he renews my inner being and empowers me with all his gifts. He brings me into the fullness of life that God has planned for mankind, the life of love. And finally he gives me permission to be me—to be myself, to be human, to be divine, to make mistakes, to rise to the heights of greatness.

And with Jesus' concern, the Father's love, and the Spirit's power I am not afraid to return to the road of life and see what I will become, for I do not walk it alone. God is with me.

This is the process that happens through inner healing—Jesus' daily concern bringing me into the circle of the Father's acceptance, and their giving to me the Spirit who empowers me unto greatness and freedom. How precisely does this happen? What does the prayer "look like"? It is very simple, and it is based on the prayer of loving faith we learned about earlier. It is a way of taking this prayer we use for physical healing and applying it to the emotional and spiritual dimensions of our lives.

The Inner Healing Prayer

I pray for guidance, for faith, and for love. I renew my commitment to forgiveness, and I thank God for the person for whom I am praying, whether it is myself or another. Then, based on the facts I know about the painful situation that needs healing, I do one of two things: I go back in time and try to see and "pray forth" the way in which Jesus was ministering to that person at the time he was hurt; or, if it is more appropriate to the kind of hurt for which I am praying, I allow my imagination to be led by the Holy Spirit to find an image or a symbol of the inner pain of the person, and I try to see the way in which Jesus is ministering to that pain and "pray forth" the healing image. In one of these ways, then, I ask to be a channel of Jesus' healing love to the person in need, that through my faith, love and prayer Jesus can heal the memory. Jesus does not take the memory away; rather he renders the pain associated with it helpless to hurt us, so that it can be the foundation of a new strength within us, e.g., compassion.

An example of the first way was given in the previous chapter—the woman whose fears of leaving the house went back to a childhood voyage. In this situation, under the guidance of the Spirit, and after I had listened attentively to her story, I saw in my imagination as vividly as I could the ship, the water, her parents, and the little girl with Jesus ever at her side doing for her the things her parents ought to have done for her but could not for whatever reason. In faith I know that what my imagination was seeing somehow actually happened: Jesus had ministered to that little girl, and this prayer was helping her to accept his love so that it could free her of her fear. As we remember Dr. Penfield's research, we realize that this kind of prayer has its basis in scientific fact.

An example of the second way would be this: in praying for a person who is depressed, to see that person's depressed personality as a barren desert with a cloud cover of gloom overcast in the sky, but then to see life breaking through. The sun slowly eats up the clouds just as it does in real life—the sun symbolizing the Son. A river of living water courses its way through the desert bringing new possibilities of life. The gentle breath of the Spirit blows across the land bringing with it the seeds of plants and trees and flowers. Then all the seeds grow, and the desert becomes a verdant valley in which the animals feel free to take residence and add their own life to the scene. Finally, the person himself, arm in arm with Jesus, strolls through the valley taking possession of it and enjoying all its beauty.

It is important in this kind of prayer to respond to the uniqueness of the person for whom one is praying; thus it is important to learn to listen to oneself deep inside where the Spirit of God dwells. From there he will guide our prayer to touch those hurting parts of the person in need. He will bring

forth images that will touch the person deeply, even archetyp-
ally.

In the beginning as we are learning to pray in this way we
may want to imitate another who has had some experience, for
this kind of praying is strange to many of us and therefore not
a little difficult. This reaction is normal and we should not
judge ourselves as incompetent just because we do not feel
entirely confident in our first attempts. If, by imitating some
of the styles of prayer we read in a book or hear from someone
else's lips, we reach out and help another or ourselves, that is
good. Often, at first, it is enough that we have the faith to
reach out and offer to pray that Jesus would heal, let alone also
to have original words for our prayers. In time the Spirit will
lead us to our own individual way of praying if we continue to
be open to him. For the essence of this prayer is heart touching
heart with love; into that situation Jesus can enter freely with
his divine and infinite love.

There are many images with which we can begin to respond to the hurts and needs of others. If the person we are
praying with was hurt by another in a particular situation, we
can recreate that situation imaginatively but with Jesus
there—as he indeed was—and let him minister to each person, forgiving one, protecting another, comforting and assist-
ing all who need him. If the hurt we are praying about comes
more from a general relationship with another than from one
single event, we can call the other person into mind standing
before us but seeing Jesus between us and that person, taking
into himself all the hurt, aggression, and anger that passed
between us—as he already has on the cross—and only allowing the love that we have shared to pass through him to touch
each other. Sometimes the hurts of the past are most easily
imagined as chains around a person or a prison that cages him
in, and the prayer of inner healing is one in which we see Jesus
breaking those bonds and leading the person into a new land of
freedom and wholeness and productivity.

The images of life related here, while not referring to anything physically real, refer to a deeper, spiritual level of reality which we understand only vaguely—the realm of the unconscious and the Spirit. They do not describe literally what is happening, but rather figuratively, imaginatively. While all this may seem to some to be child's play, the childlikeness of it all has led many into the kingdom. Remembering what was said earlier about the power of the imagination, this kind of prayer makes perfect sense. However inadequate our form of prayer may be or the style we use, Jesus looks not to externals but to our love and our faith—our faith in him to heal us. He will use whatever paltry means we can put at his disposal.

So we ask simply, we ask imaginatively, we ask lovingly, we ask in faith. Jesus wants to heal us; it will be done. Thus we conclude by thanking God for his gift, and by asking God to protect the delicate and sensitive inner being of the person for whom we are praying until he feels the total strength of the healing.

In this kind of prayer, Jesus takes from our memory and personal unconscious all the hurt and pain, leaving the memory of the situation powerless to affect the present in a negative way. Jesus can do this because, as we have learned in previous chapters, he has already done it on the cross and in his resurrection. That is where the real work of inner healing and inner transformation has been done; in prayer we only accept and apply to ourselves the gift we were given long ago.

Because God's love is an historical fact, because the transformation of all human nature and therefore of my own human nature is an historical fact, I can have complete and relaxed confidence as I pray for inner healing. I am only praying for what I already have. I am praying that my eyes will be opened to see the gift before me and that in my heart I will accept it with humble gratitude.

I can relax in my prayer also because it is Jesus' responsibility to see that healing takes place, not mine. The more I place my own desires, my own expectations, my own thoughts and feelings out of control of the situation (not that I do not have to deal with and recognize these parts of me, but they are not to be in *control*), the more Jesus will be in control; and that is the best situation for all concerned, for only Jesus can heal.

It is my duty, however, as a child of God when praying for myself, and as a minister in Jesus' name when I am praying for another, that my prayer reflect in all its aspects the attitude of Jesus toward the person for whom I am praying. This *is* my responsibility. The reason it is necessary to reflect Christ is that the more clearly I am like him in prayer the more completely he can use me as a channel of his healing love to the person in need. Even when I am that person in need, to have attitudes toward myself and my problems unlike Christ's attitudes will prevent me from receiving, to some degree, the grace of his healing love, at least at that time.

Over and over again the Scriptures have told us one truth: Jesus loves every part of us. We can hear that said so often, however, that we can forget what it means, and we need to have the definition of love spelled out for us so that we can understand how Jesus feels toward us. At these times St. Paul's definition of love can be helpful, for if Jesus is love and if he loves us, this definition applies to him most of all.

Love [and therefore also Jesus] is always patient and kind . . . never jealous . . . never boastful or conceited . . . never rude or selfish . . . does not take offense . . . is not resentful . . . takes no pleasure in other people's sins but delights in the truth . . . is always ready to excuse, to trust, to hope, and to endure whatever comes (1 Cor 13:4-7).

This is what it means that Jesus loves us; and so, as we try to bring the love of Jesus to others or even to ourselves in the ministry of inner healing, our attitudes need to reflect these qualities. Instead of reading the word "love" at the beginning of that passage, we can place the petition, "Lord, change me that I might be. . . ." For especially in the time of counseling and prayer with another, we need to let Jesus shine through us.

Practical Advice

We need to take our time in listening and praying. People need time to tell their problems, but, even more, they need to be given time to feel loved and accepted just as they are. When we can give people the time they need and listen to them patiently and attentively, we are already bringing them the love of Jesus. In the prayer also, time is often needed to be open to the Spirit's guidance, to pray forth the images of healing imaginatively, and to allow the person for whom we are praying to respond emotionally to the prayer. The prayer ought not to be rushed, and a time and place should be chosen for this kind of prayer, keeping these needs in mind.

The opposite of a loving attitude is a judgmental one. Since Christ loves us, we know that he does not judge us or condemn us (Rom 8:1); therefore the minister of inner healing needs to have non-judgmental ways about him. Also, Jesus is never unforgiving, depressing, retaliative, pushy, cynical, or fearful, and a minister of healing who would act in these ways would be doing Jesus an injustice. Rather, when we pray with another we can be gentle and care for the person, even allowing ourselves to feel the hurt with them, for this may encourage them to totally let go of their hurt. Another way of saying this is that we need to listen to people in an open and non-judgmental way, praying with them out of understanding for their situation with real compassion in our heart for their hurt.

Sometimes we do find ourselves, even against our wills, judging another person for having a particular kind of problem. This automatic reaction can be a signal to us that we need healing for a similar problem ourselves. For nothing would trigger an automatic response like that except a projection, i.e., seeing in another a problem that we have in ourselves but one that we do not desire to face openly. When we meet another with a similar problem we immediately dislike him because first we have unconsciously judged ourselves as bad for having this problem.

Our automatic responses can tell us much about ourselves. If we find ourselves in a prayer situation with these feelings, we can be aware of their origin and therefore prevent ourselves from acting unkindly toward the person we are trying to help. Then, later, we can find someone to talk with and pray with to uncover the reason for our surprising reaction.

An example of this situation came to me from a woman whom I know to be a beautiful minister of healing. She began talking with another woman one day whose problem was that she had had an abortion and she felt guilty about it even many years later. My friend found a surprising and sudden reaction of disgust and anger within her as this woman told of her problem and her pain over it, for while she had never approved of other people's wrongdoing, she always had been able to identify with them in their hurt and shame. She controlled her feelings, however, and prayed with the lady to help her feel God's love and forgiveness again.

Later she went to a friend for help. In conversation she recalled that her own mother had attempted to abort her but failed, and she realized that she had not forgiven her mother for this attack on her life and had pushed all of her feelings of anger into her unconscious where the Lord could not heal them. In prayer she was able to forgive her mother and accept the Lord's protection around her and within her, healing her of the effects of that attack. It is important, then, to pay attention to our feelings as we walk through life with Jesus so that he is free to heal us and can make us open channels of his love to others. The experience of his love will open our heart to have compassion for others.

This is the reason that, while reading, lectures, and workshops can be helpful in the process of learning how to pray inner healing for ourselves and for others, we really learn not by any form of "head knowledge" but rather by knowledge of the heart, i.e., experience. We learn how to pray by being prayed with, or at least by hearing or reading the prayer of another, and then by doing, i.e., prayer for inner healing over and over again. Nonetheless, God in his power and wisdom has stirred hearts with this ability to be sensitive and faith-full through private prayer. But I have not seen that to be his ordinary way. However, once a person has understood the basics, God takes over in his heart to guide him into his own unique insights into the inner healing process.

It is also well after praying for inner healing to spend some time—it does not have to be a long period—in personal prayer to be cleansed of the other person's hurt which a minister would feel as he empathized with another in need, or to be refreshed and renewed before he would go forth into the relative harshness of the world. This practical suggestion is a safety device so that we will not allow the world to infringe upon that sensitive part of us that we should only entrust to Jesus.

It is well to remember also that, since the changes we seek healing for in inner healing originate deep in our psyche, it may very well take some time for changes in our actual behavior to appear. It is common for many people first experiencing inner healing not to feel the full effects of the prayer for several days. This reaction may simply be due to the fact that most people are not accustomed to having their hurts and problems handled with so much love and gentleness, and it takes several days to accept it all as real.

But the deep-rooted changes in feeling, attitude, and behavior that we seek take much time to unfold. After all, it took years for the problems we have to grow, and over the years these problems have developed the strength of habits; so it would not seem unlikely that it would take weeks or months or maybe sometimes even years for a healing to take place, revealing itself a little at a time. But during this period of changing we can be consoled: for Jesus is taking time for *our* sakes, so that we will not be shocked in the change, so that we can have the dignity of being a part of the change, and so that he can heal every underlying part of the problem perfectly and in just the right order, not quickly and in a slipshod manner as we might want it just to obtain an immediate effect. And every step of the way Jesus has a dual motive—if I can presume to speak personally for him: he wants to see the real, effective healing take place, and he also wants us to become closer to him in friendship, so that when the healing is completed we will have a more intimate understanding of each other and a stronger partnership through life.

That is the great personal reward of practicing inner healing: we will come to understand how deep and how high and how wide is God's infinite love for us. We will find that he is our best friend and strongest ally.

Nothing therefore can come between us and the love of Christ, even if we are troubled or worried, or being persecuted, or lacking food or clothes, or being threatened or even attacked. As Scripture promised: For your sake we are being massacred daily, and reckoned as sheep for the slaughter. These are the trials through which we triumph, by the power of him who loved us. For I am certain of this: neither death nor life, no angel, no prince, nothing that exists, nothing still to come, not any power, or height or depth, not any created thing, can ever come between us and the love of God made visible in Christ Jesus our Lord (Rom 8:35-39).

Chapter VIII
A Prayer for Inner Healing

The Lord Jesus is the center of the inner healing prayer, so as we prepare now to pray to him, we need to find a place where we can be comfortable and quiet in order to keep our minds on him who heals us. We also need a sufficient amount of time so that we can pray imaginatively and thoroughly, and so that after the prayer we have time to settle into ourselves and come out of the depth of prayer without a jolt. Thirty to sixty minutes is a good time to allot for this prayer.

We do not have to be overly concerned with our emotional reaction or lack of it during or after the prayer. Sometimes the healing touch of the Lord is signified by deep emotions and emotional outpourings like crying; at other times Jesus heals us deeply without any emotional display. So whichever happens, simply accept and believe. Whether or not we react emotionally, however, a time of quiet after the prayer is always suggested, if for nothing else than for thanksgiving.

While I have heard of people who pray this prayer in proxy for another, this has not been my experience. Ordinarily, if we are to pray for another, we need to enlist his cooperation, since free will is so much of the essence of yielding our hurts to the love of Christ. The prayer printed here is mainly meant for the reader to pray for himself or herself, although images from it could be adapted for a prayer in ministry to another. Obviously, this is not the only format or wording of an inner healing prayer, for the prayer is a totally imaginative and creative one. Rather, I hope that using this prayer will help readers to develop their own way to pray for inner healing for themselves and others.

In this prayer we will cover, in general ways, many, although not all, kinds of situations in which people are hurt in life. If a particular part of the prayer applies to us directly and strongly, we can stay with that part, making as vivid in our imagination as we can the circumstances that need healing and especially the loving presence of Christ in that situation with us. Even if we leave the printed prayer and go off with the Lord into a situation from our past, we stay with the situation until some kind of release seems to happen. For we trust that the Holy Spirit is guiding this prayer to meet our individual needs, and every time we pray this prayer something new and wonderful can happen. After that particular memory has been healed, we can return to the prayer and continue on.

If a part of the prayer does not apply to us—and of necessity one may be interspersed throughout this prayer—pass over it and move on to the next part.

If a particular memory that comes back is so painful that we doubt we can handle it alone, it may be best to set it aside and find someone who can pray with us about it later. On the other hand, if at the revelation of this memory we concentrate on the loving presence of Jesus with us, we will be able to get through many situations that at first seemed insurmountable.

With these thoughts in mind, it is time to pray. First, let us relax, become comfortable, and breathe deeply. Closing our eyes for a moment, let us remember that we are always in the presence of our God and that we are always surrounded by his love.

Prayer for Inner Healing

"Thank you, Jesus, for your love for me. Thank you for being with me here right now, and throughout every minute of my life. Thank you that your desire is to heal me of the hurt and pain and confusion of my life. I need you so much, Jesus, and you are so good to me. I give you praise for being God and thanks for being near me.

"I ask you to stir your Spirit within me, Lord, to guide this prayer, to release from deep within me only the memories that you see ought to be healed now. I ask you, Jesus, to increase my faith in you at this moment, my hope for a renewed life, and my love for you and for myself—help me through this prayer to see and love myself as you see and love me, Jesus. And give to me all the gifts I need to pray the perfect prayer you want prayed for me right now.

"Lord, I also want to renew my commitment to forgive at this moment all who have wronged me, and I ask that a special measure of your forgiving love may flow through me during this prayer to all the people who have hurt me in the situations I will pray about today. Thank you, Jesus, that all this happens just because I ask for it.

Parents

"Lord Jesus, I thank you for my parents and for the life they gave to me. It was all a gift from you, Lord, and especially if I have never before thanked you for the gift of my life, I do that right now.

"But, Jesus, you know that I did not always feel loved by my parents. Sometimes I was closed to them, sometimes they to me. Sometimes they could have changed things; sometimes they couldn't change anything because of the limitations in their own lives. Jesus, I ask you to come into those relationships right now. I ask you to heal the hurt I have carried with me from my childhood and to free me to be myself.

"Jesus, I thank you that, as I imagine my mother standing before me, I see you between us, uniting us in all the ways that we were good for each other, but separating and protecting us in all the ways our relationship was harmful to either of us. I thank you, Jesus, that you have been with me since my first moment of life in my mother's womb, and that the light of your love filled and surrounded even that first single cell of life. I thank you that you remained with me, loving me, protecting me, keeping me company in my mother's womb.

"I thank you that you protected me against any disturbance or attack while I was there defenseless and helpless. I see your light around me so powerfully, Jesus, that it consumes the darkness of any evil that would come to harm me. If my parents had any negative feelings about my coming into the world, I ask you, Jesus, to heal any effect those feelings have had on me. If at any time during my stay in my mother's womb my mother hurt herself in any way, if she was hurt by anyone else, if she ever took the wrong medicine or in any way abused her own body, if she experienced any severe emotional strain, I ask you to protect me from the negative feelings about life and about myself that these could have caused in me, and I thank you that you are healing all of these problems right now.

"I thank you, Jesus, that you are with me at my birth, that you give me permission to be myself, and that you have a plan for my life that gives me a direction and a dignity I could never have in any other way. Thank you, Jesus, for being so proud of me at the time of my birth, and for thanking the Father yourself for my life. Thank you for promising to remain with me every day during my life.

"Jesus, in my relationship with my mother, I ask you to enter all those special areas of conflict that we had and heal them. I ask you to come to me in every circumstance that I needed her love but she was not able to give it for whatever reason, and if any particular situation comes to mind now, I ask you to be with me in a special way. . . . Help me, Jesus, to forgive her all the hurt that she has caused in my life, and I ask for forgiveness for all the ways I have hurt her. And, Lord, if my mother was largely absent from my life, whether that was due to illness or death, to my parents' separating, or to her working to help support the family, comfort that part of me that still needs a mother, that still looks for a mother's tender care and gentle touch, and fill that place within me that aches to find a deeply accepting love. Fill that place with your love, Jesus, so that it will not ache any longer. Thank you, Jesus, for your love for me.

"Lord, I thank you for my father and for all the ways he loved me, especially when I was a child; but his love was not perfect, Jesus, because that is the way things are in this world. As I see him in my imagination standing before me, I thank you, Jesus, that you are standing between us, taking into yourself everything in our relationship that was harmful to either of us and magnifying and perfecting the love that we have shared.

"I ask you to protect me, Jesus, from any negative feelings my father has ever had toward me, especially if he did not want me to be born or if he ever judged me as an inadequate child. Right now, Lord, I ask you to help me give up any resentments I have held toward him; let me join in your forgiveness for him. And I seek to be forgiven for all the things I have ever done that hurt him. If any particular moments come to mind at this time, I ask you to help me see you as you were there in that moment, loving and forgiving us both, and help me to feel your presence in a special way. . . .

"Lord Jesus, I ask you to be in every part of my heart that aches to have my father's love still. For whatever reason in his own life, Jesus, my father was not always there when I needed him, was not always strong and understanding, firm and gentle, kind and mature. How I needed him to be all of those things! You be them for me, Jesus. Sit me on your knee and let me feel close to you and protected by your strength. I thank you that you feel free to share with me your deep feelings of love and affection for me, that you are not too big or too important to play games with me and enter my world, to love me at my level. Thank you, Jesus, that you take me with you to do things and that you teach me the things I needed to learn from my father that he couldn't teach me. Thank you for telling me how beautiful or handsome I am in your eyes.

"Jesus, if my father was ever cruel to me physically or verbally, I thank you that at those moments you took the scars of that brutality into your own heart because you want me to be free from them. Thank you, Jesus, for taking my place and loving me in the midst of that confusing situation. Your love strengthens me to have confidence in myself again, in my lovability and my inner worth. Your perfect love for me heals this wound, and I feel acceptable and able to be equal again with other human beings.

Family

"Jesus, in a similar way, I ask you to be with me now as I call to mind the other members of my family—brothers, sisters, aunts, uncles, grandparents, cousins, and even pets. I ask that your forgiveness flow through us so that we can give up any family squabbles or feuds and be healed of all the pain we have caused each other through misunderstanding, ignorance, or cruelty. I ask that you touch the parts of my heart that have been hardened toward members of my family by hurt, and that you soften me by loving those parts of me that I might be open again. And if any particular situation or relationship comes to mind now, I ask that your love stay with me in a special way so that I may take the time to let you heal my broken heart. . . .

"Lord, if my problem with family was their absence, I ask you to fill the loneliness in my heart now with your presence. Especially if I was an only child, or if a dear grandparent, aunt or uncle died when I was young, I ask you to help me see you with me as my older brother, wise, loving, gentle, and always ready to be with me. Be my constant companion and fill the emptiness of my childhood with your love.

"If as a child I suffered a loss through the death of a

member of my family, or even of a dear pet whom I cared about with great affection, be with me at the time of that death to explain to me what has happened in words I can understand. Hold me close, Jesus, and let me cry out my sorrow on your shoulder, sitting in your lap. Remain with me during those awful and desolate days afterward so that your love will bring brightness into my heart again. Thank you, Jesus, for your love. Let me stay here with you for a while to feel it deeply. . . .

School and Friends

"Jesus, how difficult the transition from home to school was—how exciting, confusing, and scary. All the new people and all the new buildings and all the expectations that were placed upon me—how upsetting this new world was! Lord, you were with me the first day I went to school; help me to see you with me there and to feel the comfortableness of your presence.

"There were so many people to get along with, Jesus, and with some of them I didn't succeed too well. Teachers, students, friends—all at one time or another caused me trouble and hurt. Thank you, Jesus, for bringing to mind the people I need to forgive from my school days. Walk with me through each classroom and down each hallway, and help me to forgive every person I meet there who hurt me. Especially teachers who made me feel inadequate or incompetent and classmates who made a fool of me or who did their best to make me feel stupid—help me to remember them now, Lord, and to let go of my resentments by allowing your forgiveness to flow through me to them. . . . And forgive me, Lord, for all the times I hurt teachers or students in my school.

"Lord, if I was ever too severely punished in school, help me to see you there with me taking the punishment and all the scars that came from it into yourself, leaving me free to be me. Help me to see your love for me and that you know I do not deserve such treatment, and help me to accept your belief in me more completely than that adult's disapproval. Thank you, Jesus, for taking that punishment for me in your own passion and death, and for helping me to feel the effects of your saving love in this situation.

The Church

"Lord Jesus, I come to you now and ask you to help me to be reconciled to your Church and to your representatives who pastor your flock. Lord, I have been hurt and deeply disappointed by their failings and weaknesses. Thank you for staying with me, Jesus, to help me in this area.

"Jesus, I ask you to help me forgive any priest or minister, any sister, brother, or catechism teacher who has ever misrepresented your word to me. Thank you, Jesus, for the gift of forgiveness for them, for I ask you to help me let go of all the things I hold against them. Especially if they have damaged very personal areas of my life by giving me bad advice, by talking to me in a condemning tone, or by hurting my feelings, I ask that your healing love enter those wounds and heal them now. Lord, sometimes many years of pain and distance from you have been caused by one mistake; thank you for healing the pain of that distance and for helping me to forgive the one who caused it.

"Sometimes, Lord, great pain has been caused by rigid laws in your Church, and by rigid application of laws. Help me to forgive the Church in its humanness and sinfulness for making me feel excluded, second class, or inferior for not being able to measure up to standards set by human beings and not by you. Thank you, Jesus, that your love fills the wounds in my heart with a healing balm, so that I can feel close to you again. And help me to forgive, Lord, the brokenness of your Christian Church and all the pain that disunity has caused me. Forgive me, too, for any way in which I have contributed to animosity among Christian brothers and sisters.

"Jesus, if there is a special hurt involving the Church that you want to heal in me right now, I ask you to bring it into my mind and to stay with me in your love that I may be free. . . .

A Special Gift

"Jesus, I thank you for the many gifts you have given me during my life and for the gifts you have already given me during this prayer. I thank you that I see you standing before me, that I now see you kneeling before me—you, my Lord and my God—because you want to be my servant. You want to give me a special gift today, one that is unique to me, one that I have needed or wanted for a long time. In your hands I see a treasure box, and you place that box in my lap. I thank you, Jesus, from the depths of my heart as I open that box and accept the gift inside that is for me. . . . How special you are, how generous, how kind! Thank you, Jesus for being so desirous of making me happy, and thank you for the specialness of this gift. In the days and weeks to come teach me through prayer and through life's experiences how to use this gift for your greater glory. How much I owe to you, Lord! My whole life and the very fact that it is livable is a gift from you; every talent, ability, need, relationship, and experience comes from your love to make me happy.

Conclusion

"So, thank you, Lord, for everything. Thank you for healing the hurting parts of my life so that they will never hurt in that terrible and lonely way again. Thank you for being tender with me and for being kind enough to forgive my faults and failures in the situations you have touched today. Thank you for your overwhelming love which is ever with me, whether I am conscious of it or not.

"I ask you, Jesus, that your peace would settle in me, and especially protect all the parts of me you have healed today. Grant that a calmness may fill those parts of my being with an assurance that life can and will be abundant, that things can and will be new, because *you* can make things different.

"I pray, too, for those whom I have forgiven and from whom I have needed forgiveness—may they feel the freedom that comes from the forgiveness that originates in your heart. And guide me, Jesus, to know whether it would be kind and good to seek out those from whom I need forgiveness to receive it from them face-to-face. And if that is your plan, give me the courage and the humility to follow through on your desire, that I may be totally free.

"I love you, Jesus. I thank you and praise you for being God, for being a God who cares and who helps. I thank you for knowing me as I am and for planning this moment from all eternity—a moment when you and I would become closer than ever before by your sharing my weakness. Thank you for showing me our Father's love and for empowering me with the gifts of your Spirit. Show me how to walk always in your presence, in your healing light, that my path may lead me straight to you. Amen."